CW01304548

Bookkeeping and Accounting

The Ultimate Guide to Basic Bookkeeping and Basic Accounting Principles for Small Business

© **Copyright 2017**

All rights Reserved. No part of this book may be reproduced in any form without permission in writing from the author. Reviewers may quote brief passages in reviews.

Disclaimer: No part of this publication may be reproduced or transmitted in any form or by any means, mechanical or electronic, including photocopying or recording, or by any information storage and retrieval system, or transmitted by email without permission in writing from the publisher.

While all attempts have been made to verify the information provided in this publication, neither the author nor the publisher assume any responsibility for errors, omissions or contrary interpretations of the subject matter herein.

Any persons or organizations referred to herein are composites for the purpose of illustration and do not represent real persons or organizations.

This book is for entertainment purposes only. The views expressed are those of the author alone, and should not be taken as expert instruction or commands. The reader is responsible for his or her own actions.

Adherence to all applicable laws and regulations, including international, federal, state and local laws governing professional licensing, business practices, advertising and all other aspects of doing business in the US, Canada, UK or any other jurisdiction is the sole responsibility of the purchaser or reader.

Neither the author nor the publisher assumes any responsibility or liability whatsoever on the behalf of the purchaser or reader of these materials. Any perceived slight of any individual or organization is purely unintentional.

Contents

PART 1: BOOKKEEPING 10

THE ULTIMATE GUIDE TO BOOKKEEPING FOR SMALL BUSINESS 10

INTRODUCTION 11

CHAPTER 1 – BOOKKEEPING BASICS 13

    DOUBLE-ENTRY METHOD 13

    SOURCE DOCUMENTS 13

    END-OF-PERIOD PROCEDURES 14

    COMPILE THE ADJUSTED TRIAL BALANCE 16

    CLOSING THE BOOKS 17

    PREPARING REPORTS 17

CHAPTER 2 – WHAT'S NEW IN BOOKKEEPING FOR SMALL BUSINESS? 19

    OPEN A BUSINESS BANK ACCOUNT 19

    CHOOSE THE BEST BOOKKEEPING SOFTWARE FOR YOUR BUSINESS 19

    CREATE A LOGO 27

    MONTHLY BOOKKEEPING REPORTS 28

    HIRE EMPLOYEES 28

    TRY NEW SYSTEMS 28

    BE HANDS-ON WITH YOUR BOOKKEEPER 29

    OUTSOURCE TO A BOOKKEEPER 29

CHAPTER 3 – MANAGING ASSETS, LIABILITIES AND OWNER'S EQUITY 31

    ASSETS 31

    Owner's Equity 35

CHAPTER 4 – USING LEDGERS AND JOURNALS TO TRACK BUSINESS ACTIVITY 36

    Financial Journals 36

        Cash Receipts Journal (CRJ) 37

        Cash Payments Journal (CPJ) 38

        Sales Journal (SJ) 39

        Sales Returns Journal (SRL) 39

        Purchases Journal (PJ) 40

        Purchases Returns Journal (PRJ) 40

        General Journal (GJ) 41

    The Ledgers 42

        General Ledger (GL) 42

        Accounts Receivable Ledger (ARL) and Accounts Payable Ledger (APL) 43

    Tracking Transactions 43

CHAPTER 5 – EMPLOYEES 45

    Get an Employer Identification Number (EIN) 46

    Find out whether you need state or local tax IDs 46

    Decide if you want an independent contractor or an employee 46

    Ensure new employees return a completed W-4 form 47

    Schedule pay periods to coordinate tax withholding for IRS 47

    Create a compensation plan for holidays, vacation and leave 47

    Choose an in-house or external service for administrating payroll 48

    Decide who will manage your payroll system 48

    Know which records must stay on file and for how long 49

    Report payroll taxes as needed on a quarterly and annual basis 49

    Setting-Up Direct Deposit 51

    Employee Benefits 51

        Required Benefits 51

        Optional Benefits 52

CHAPTER 6 – DEPRECIATION 53

    Book Depreciation 54

    Tax Depreciation 55

CHAPTER 7 – ADJUSTING ENTRIES 56

ASSET ACCOUNTS 56

ADJUSTING ENTRIES – LIABILITY ACCOUNTS 59

CHAPTER 8 – MAKING SENSE OUT OF THE FINANCIAL STATEMENTS 61

THE BALANCE SHEET 61

THE INCOME STATEMENT 64

STATEMENT OF OWNER'S EQUITY 65

STATEMENT OF CASH FLOW 66

CHAPTER 9 – TAXES FOR SMALL BUSINESSES 69

OTHER TAX DEDUCTIONS 72

PREPARING W-2'S FOR YOUR EMPLOYEES 74

CHAPTER 10 – SMALL BUSINESS CHECKLIST 77

CHAPTER 11 – BOOKKEEPING TIPS FOR YOUR SMALL BUSINESS 79

TIP 1: KEEP ACCURATE RECORDS 79

TIP 2: SORT AND FILE RECEIPTS 79

TIP 3: COLLECT APPLICABLE TAXES 80

TIP 4: DO ACCURATE INVOICING 80

TIP 5: GET DONATION AND CONTRIBUTION RECEIPTS 80

TIP 6: SCHEDULE PROFIT AND LOSS STATEMENTS 81

CONCLUSION 82

PART 2: ACCOUNTING 83

THE ULTIMATE GUIDE TO ACCOUNTING FOR BEGINNERS – LEARN THE BASIC ACCOUNTING PRINCIPLES 83

INTRODUCTION 84

CHAPTER 1 - ACCOUNTING IS DIFFERENT FROM BOOKKEEPING 85

CHAPTER 2 - UNDERSTANDING THE VOCABULARY 87

CHAPTER 3 – ACCOUNTING REPORTS: THE INCOME STATEMENT 89

CHAPTER 4 - THE BALANCE SHEET 94

CHAPTER 5 – THE CASH FLOW STATEMENT 100

CHAPTER 6 – THE ACCOUNTING EQUATION 103

CHAPTER 7 – THE CPA AND PUBLIC ACCOUNTING 105

CHAPTER 8 – JOBS IN ACCOUNTING: FINANCIAL ACCOUNTING 107

CHAPTER 9 – TAX ACCOUNTING 110

CHAPTER 10 – ACCOUNTING CONSULTANTS 112

- Chapter 11 - Forensic Accounting ... 114
- Chapter 12 - Personal Accounting ... 116
- Chapter 13 – Measures and Ratios ... 117
- Chapter 14 – Accounting Software ... 122
- Chapter 15 - Time Value of Money - Present Value Concepts ... 124
- Conclusion ... 129

PART 3: ACCOUNTING ... 135

AN ESSENTIAL GUIDE TO LEARNING ACCOUNTING QUICKLY ... 135

INTRODUCTION ... 136

CHAPTER 1 – GENERALLY ACCEPTED ACCOUNTING PRINCIPLES (GAAP) ... 137
- Financial Accounting Foundation (FAF) ... 138
- What are the Qualities of the GAAP? ... 139

CHAPTER 2 – THE ACCOUNTING EQUATION ... 140

CHAPTER 3 – CASH METHOD VS ACCRUAL METHOD ... 142

CHAPTER 4 – DOUBLE-ENTRY ACCOUNTING ... 145
- Debits and Credits ... 146
- T Accounts ... 147

CHAPTER 5 – FINANCIAL STATEMENTS ... 149
- Trial Balance ... 149
- Income Statement ... 149
- Statement of Retained Earnings ... 150
- The Balance Sheet ... 151

CHAPTER 6 – MAKING ADJUSTING ENTRIES ... 153
- Prepaid Expense ... 153
- Depreciation Expense ... 153
- Unearned Revenue ... 154
- Accrued Expense ... 154
- Accrued Revenue ... 154

CHAPTER 7 – COMPLETING THE ACCOUNTING CYCLE ... 155
- The Worksheet ... 155
- Closing Entries ... 157
- Types of Closing Entries ... 158

CHAPTER 8 – SPECIAL JOURNALS ... 159

ACCOUNTS RECEIVABLE 160

ACCOUNTS PAYABLE 161

FIXED ASSETS LEDGER AND THE PROPERTY, PLANT, AND EQUIPMENT (PPE) ACCOUNT 162

SALES JOURNAL 162

CASH RECEIPTS JOURNAL 163

PURCHASES JOURNAL 164

CASH DISBURSEMENTS JOURNAL 165

GENERAL JOURNAL TRANSACTIONS 165

CHAPTER 9 – ACCOUNTS RECEIVABLES 167

ACCOUNTS RECEIVABLE 167

NOTES RECEIVABLE 168

METHODS FOR UNCOLLECTIBLE ACCOUNTS 168

FINANCIAL STATEMENT PRESENTATION 170

MATURITY DATE 170

INTEREST INCOME 171

CHAPTER 10 – LIABILITIES AND PAYROLL 173

KNOWN LIABILITIES 173

ESTIMATED LIABILITIES 174

EMPLOYEE BENEFITS 175

CONTINGENT LIABILITIES 175

CHAPTER 11 – CURRENT AND LONG-TERM ASSETS 177

CASH 177

SHORT-TERM INVESTMENTS 178

TRADE ACCOUNTS RECEIVABLE 179

FIXED ASSETS 180

DEPRECIATION 181

CHAPTER 12 – OWNER'S EQUITY 184

SOME DIFFERENCES BETWEEN SOLE PROPRIETORSHIP AND CORPORATION EQUITY 184

RECORDING FOR DIFFERENT COMPANY TYPES 185

PARTNERSHIPS 187

CHAPTER 13 – INCOME STATEMENT 189

REVENUE 189

SALES AND REVENUE 190

EXPENSES	190
OPERATING EXPENSES	190
CHAPTER 14 – STATEMENT OF CASH FLOWS	**192**
HOW IS THE STATEMENT OF CASH FLOWS USED?	193
METHODS OF CASH FLOWS REPORTING	194
OPERATING ACTIVITIES	195
INVESTING ACTIVITIES	196
FINANCING ACTIVITIES	196
CHAPTER 15 – FINANCIAL RATIOS	**199**
PROFIT RATIOS	199
DEBT RATIOS	200
EFFICIENCY RATIOS	200
EQUITY RATIOS	200
LIQUIDITY RATIOS	201
CONCLUSION	**202**

Part 1: Bookkeeping

The Ultimate Guide to Bookkeeping for Small Business

Introduction

Whether you are just starting your business or have had your business for years, it is important to know bookkeeping.

Bookkeeping has been around for centuries. However, it has evolved over time to better help your business keep track of your finances.

Bookkeeping covers a long list of aspects that help the business owner make decisions about the company. To better understand bookkeeping, my goal is to help you get a good feel for knowing how to read the financial reports, the basics of bookkeeping, employees, understanding the balance sheet and income statement, and so much more.

Come along with me as we explore the world of bookkeeping and help you, the business owner, understand how to make sense out of bookkeeping.

As an added bonus, I have included a section for your business taxes. I also included a step-by-step process of preparing W-2 forms and the information that is needed for those. You will soon find out that there is more to it than just providing the information and typing it up on the W-2 form.

Keep reading and you will see what it takes to get on the same page as your bookkeeper. I always said, "It is not the business owner that runs the business. It is the business owner teamed up with the bookkeeper that truly runs the business."

Running a business can be fun and rewarding. However, if you do not have the basic knowledge of the fundamental financial skills needed, it can prove to be stressful as well.

Throughout this book you will learn the basics of bookkeeping and finding the right bookkeeper for you. As you go through it, you will also learn about the ledgers and journals. It is important that you know where your money is at all times. I also take the time to talk to you about hiring employees. Let's face it, if your business is going to grow above a certain level, you will eventually need to hire someone to work with you.

There is also a lot of software available to help you with all your bookkeeping needs, although not all accounting software is right for your business. We will take a look at a few of the top rated applications and give you both the good and bad of each one.

Don't forget, you also need to understand those scary financial statements. That's why we will take a look at the four main financial statements and break them down for you so that you can easily read and understand each one.

It does not matter if you have been in business for a couple of years or are just starting, you will be filing taxes at the end of the year. This is a lot of work and your bookkeeper can help you get prepared. Within the bonus chapter, I included a checklist for small businesses to help you along the way in knowing which documents you need to find and hold on to.

Did you know that as a business owner you can deduct a lot of your expenses? I included that as well. It is only a small list, and with a little research you could probably find more.

Finally, I also included, in detail, how to go about preparing, distributing, and filing the employees' W-2's.

So come along with me as we take this glorious adventure into bookkeeping for small businesses and give you the power to understand your businesses financial health.

Chapter 1 – Bookkeeping Basics

Before we get started on breaking down bookkeeping, we need to look at some of the basics. I want you to have the ability to read your financial records and understand them. This will allow for you to know the financial aspect of your business. In turn, it will allow you to make good decisions that can increase the growth of your business.

Double-Entry Method

Bookkeeping uses a method called the "Double-Entry Bookkeeping." This means that for every entry there is at least one debit and one credit.

I want you to remember this equation:

- Assets = Liabilities + Equity

This is the basic formula for the Double-Entry Method and will come into play with every transaction you make.

Source Documents

Every transaction made will have a source document. Source documents could be anything from a contract to a gas receipt. If you spent the business's money then you will need some form of proof of how much you spent. These are the source documents.

These documents will give us all the information you will need to record it in the books. This includes referencing the source documents. Some software will allow you to attach the scanned file to the transaction so that at any time you can bring up the source document.

End-Of-Period Procedures

End-of-Period Procedures relate to not only quarters. Even though all the transactions have been recorded throughout the months or year, they still are not read for preparing the financial reports.

To ensure that you have your books accurate for preparing the financial reports, you need to consider that there are procedures that need to happen at least at month-end, year-end, and the end of payroll year.

The following outline will show, as a guideline, what should be done during each time.

1. Month-End Procedures
    - Run the Company/Business Data Auditor
    - Reconcile your Bank Accounts
    - Review Reports
    - Send Customer Statements
    - Record Depreciation
    - Pay Payroll Taxes
    - Lock Periods
2. Year-End Procedures (to prepare for the new fiscal year)
    - Complete Month-End Tasks
    - Perform an Inventory Count
    - Provide Information to your Accountant
    - Enter End-of-Year Adjustments
    - Back Up your Company/Business File
    - Start New Fiscal Year
    - Optimize and Verify your Company/Business File
3. End of Payroll Year (to prepare for new fiscal year) - *NOTE: Do Not Update Tax Tables*
    - Run Your Last Payroll
    - Optimize and Verify your Company/Business File
    - Back Up your Company/Business File
    - Start a New Payroll Year
    - Install Product Updates
    - Run Your First Payroll
    - Restore Your Backup
    - Print Year-End Payroll Forms
    - Print Vendor 1099 Statements
    - Print Payroll Reports

Compile the Adjusted Trial Balance

Making these adjustments are very important. When looking at which adjustments need to be made first, you need to gather and compile a spreadsheet that will allow for your trial balance entries as well as the adjustments.

Keep in mind that these adjustments are for correcting errors in the initial trial balance so that everything will come to balance. This form for the adjustments is an internal form but will be used for helping compile the financial statements. Now that automated systems like Xero and QuickBooks are used, the trial balance worksheet is not often practiced. However, it is still a good source document. This is in part due to the automated systems creating the reports for you.

Here is an example of what the worksheet may look like:

Frank's Financials

Trial Balance

August 31, 20XX

	Unadjusted Trial Balance	Adjusted Entries	Adjusted Trial Balance
Cash	$60,000		$60,000
Accounts Receivable	$180,000	$50,000	$230,000
Inventory	$300,000		$300,000
Fixed Assets (net)	$210,000		$210,000
Accounts Payable	($90,000)		($90,000)
Accrued Liabilities	($50,000)	($25,000)	($75,000)
Notes Payable	($420,000)		($420,000)
Equity	($350,000)		($350,000)
Revenue	($400,000)	($50,000)	($450,000)
Cost of Goods Sold	$290,000		$290,000
Salaries	$200,000	$25,000	$225,000
Payroll Taxes	$20,000		$20,000
Rent	$35,000		$35,000

Other Expenses	$15,000		$15,000
Totals	$0.00	$0.00	$0.00

Closing the Books

When closing your books at the end of a fiscal year, there are 4 areas that will need to be closed. These areas are temporary accounts and should be zeroed out at the end of each fiscal year.

First, create an Income Summary account. This is considered a holding area.

Closing the Revenue Accounts

The first area that needs to be addressed are the revenue accounts. You will either Debit or Credit this account to close it out and have a zero balance. Then you will either Debit or Credit the Income Summary account to add that balance to the account. Remember if you Debit or Credit one account you must do the opposite for the other account to keep the books balanced.

Closing the Expense Accounts

The second set of accounts are the expense accounts. You will do the same with these accounts as you did with the Revenue accounts. You must close out all expense accounts.

Balancing the Income Summary

By name you should have an increase in the income summary for the revenue and a decrease for each of the expenses. Keep in mind that if the expenses are more than the revenue then it will be a negative number and considered a loss. However, if the revenue is more than the expenses then it is a gain or profit for that year.

Closing the Income Summary

The last step in closing the book is to Debit or Credit the income summary account and do the same to the Retained Earnings Account, leaving a zero balance in the income summary account.

Preparing Reports

A pretty important step is to prepare the reports or financial statements. Although there are so many reports that can be created, we are going to focus on the main reports as they are what is needed for a small business.

As a bookkeeper, you will need to get very familiar with the following reports:

- The Balance Sheet
- Income Statement

- Statement of Retained Earnings
- Statement of Cash Flow

Later in this book we will look more closely at each one of these statements and how to read them so that you can make sense out of your businesses financial standings.

Chapter 2 – What's New in Bookkeeping for Small Business?

Bookkeeping is always changing and new software is always coming out. Let's look at some of these techniques and software programs that are out there for you to use as a small business owner.

Open a Business Bank Account

You want to see your business succeed. However, how do you keep your personal finances separate from your business finances? The answer is simple; just open a business bank account.

It is extremely hard to see how your business is doing if you combine your business revenue and expenses with your personal. The best way is to check with your bank first to see if they have a business account available.

Using a spreadsheet is basic. Although, what if your business has inventory, employees, vendors, etc.? This is when an accounting or bookkeeping software could come in handy. My recommendation is QuickBooks or Xero as they both provide for these types of accounts.

Choose the Best Bookkeeping Software for your Business

Choosing a software can vary based on your needs. At minimum, you will need a ledger or cashbook. The cashbook that would include the general journal and the ledges can easily be done using a spreadsheet like Microsoft Excel or Google Sheets. Remember, Google Sheet will allow you to save it through Google and have access to the file anywhere you are.

QuickBooks and Xero may not be the best for your business. Sometimes, the most difficult part is finding the software that works the best for your needs.

Let's look at a few different bookkeeping applications that may get you started. I will include QuickBooks and Xero.

Intuit QuickBooks Online

QuickBooks Online is by far the best accounting and bookkeeping software for small businesses. I like that you can link it to your bank account. This makes it easy to use and track money when linked to your business account. It makes it easy to reconcile the business account and the books. Although there is so much more to QuickBooks Online.

Just a few of the features within QuickBooks Online include:

- Invoicing
- Expense Tracking
- Inventory Management
- Purchase Ordering
- Reporting

As your business grows, you can upgrade your account between the top three tiers. This will allow you to have everything you need for your small business. Another part that is great about QuickBooks Online is that there are apps for your phone both through Android and iOS devices. The software is also compatible with most third-party applications.

QuickBooks Online also offers some of the best pricing. There are four tiers of pricing, depending on what you need for your business. It also offers a 30-day free trial. However, if you want to just jump right into it and go for the paid versions you will get a 50% discount for the first six months. That means if you are just starting your business you will have six months to make a little extra profit and get established before you need to pay full price.

The most basic is the Self-Employed plan. This plan is $10 per month. It is designed for independent contractors and freelancers. It allows the following:

- Track Mileage
- Track Income and Expenses
- Create Invoices
- Accept Payments
- Run Reports

Keep in mind the Self-Employed plan cannot be upgraded to a higher tier. It will require you to create and set up a new account.

The next tier is the Simple Start plan. With this plan, a single user is supported and costs $15 per month. This plan includes the following:

- Track Mileage

- Track Income and Expenses
- Create Invoices
- Accept Payments
- Run Reports
- Send Estimates
- Track Sales and Sales Tax

The next tier is the Essentials plan. This plan supports multiple users and costs $35 per month. This plan includes:

- Track Mileage
- Track Income and Expenses
- Create Invoices
- Accept Payments
- Run Reports
- Send Estimates
- Track Sales and Sales Tax
- Bill Management
- Time Tracking

The last tier is the Plus plan. This plan also allows for multiple users and costs $50 per month. This plan includes:

- Track Mileage
- Track Income and Expenses
- Create Invoices
- Accept Payments
- Run Reports
- Send Estimates
- Track Sales and Sales Tax
- Bill Management
- Time Tracking

- Track Inventory
- Create Budgets
- Pay Independent Contractors that use the 1099 form

Like most small business, you will eventually have employees that you will need to pay. With QuickBooks Online, you can add this feature to any of the top three tiers for an additional monthly cost.

The best part is QuickBooks Online is very user friendly and easy to use. This software also has a good timesaving feature that you need in any good accounting and bookkeeping program. It will keep track of due dates for invoices, sync your business bank account, track your credit card transactions, and so much more. This allows you to focus more time on the business and less time on the books while maintaining accurate bookkeeping throughout your business and giving you a great outlook of the financials of the business. Another good timesaving feature that puts QuickBooks Online on top is that you can send out invoices to customers, allowing them to pay online at a click of a button.

Like with any application, things tend to go wrong with the program itself. That is why QuickBooks Online offers both phone and chat support. You can access this from the company website making it easier and quicker to get issues resolved and have you up and running again without missing a sale.

QuickBooks Online is account approved. This means that no matter what your needs are you can give your accountant access to your books. Remember, that your account will not take up a spot in your users that you give access to.

Like all programs there are some limitations, although with QuickBooks Online it seems like the sky is the limit. The limitations really lay within the mobile apps. Here are the things you can do with the mobile apps:

- Send Invoices
- Reconcile Transactions
- Take photos of receipts and attach to expenses
- View customer information and add new customers
- View dashboard data, such as account balance, profit and loss reports, and open and past due invoices.

After looking through what the app can do, if you feel like that works perfect then QuickBooks Online is the perfect software for you. However, if you prefer doing most of your accounting and bookkeeping through your phone, then there is another accounting and bookkeeping software choice for you.

Xero

If you would rather use a PC or a Mac, Xero has a lot to offer. Xero is by far the best accounting and bookkeeping software for Mac users. It easy to use and learn. What I like about Xero are the videos. Everything you do in Xero will have a video that will help you learn the software.

Xero also has comparable prices and is listed into three different plans. The starter plan is $9 per month. It does have some limitations. The features of the starter plan are:

- Unlimited Users
- Limit to Five Invoices per month
- Limit to Five Bills per month
- Limit to 20 Transaction Reconciliations per month

The standard plan is $30 per month. This includes:

- Unlimited Users
- Unlimited Invoices
- Unlimited Bills
- Unlimited Transaction Reconciliations
- Payroll for up to Five Employees

The premium plan is $70 per month. Which includes:

- Unlimited Users
- Unlimited Invoices
- Unlimited Bills
- Unlimited Transaction Reconciliations
- Payroll for up to 10 Employees. *Note: this can be adjusted to support more employees if needed.*
- Supports Multiple Currencies. *Note: this is a great feature if you do international business.*

The best part is that there are not any long-term contracts for using Xero. That means you can change at any time without having additional fees. There is also a free 30-day trial to let you try and find out if it will be the best for your business.

Much like QuickBooks Online, Xero also has many timesaving features. You can send out invoices electronically, which also allows for your customers to pay online easily. You can also turn quotes and estimates into invoices with only a few clicks. This allows for you to give a customer a quote and if they agree to go with your services you can turn that quote into an invoice and get paid.

With your business bank account linked to Xero, the system will allow you to set scheduled payments and manually pay the bills. This helps save time and ensures that all bills are paid on time and you do not need to worry about past-dues and late fees.

If you need to claim an expense that occurred, then Xero will help you to record, manage, claim, and reimburse the expense claims. You can also add expenses easily and attach the receipt images.

Xero has some great inventory management tools available for small businesses that do not offer services and instead sell merchandises that are kept in inventory. Here you can track your inventory and show how much inventory you have in stock.

As I mentioned with QuickBooks Online, it has limitations when it comes to mobile apps. Xero is one of these programs that allows for great mobile accessibility. The mobile app for Xero allows you to:

- Create and Send Invoices
- Add Receipts
- Attach Billable Expenses to Customer Invoices
- Submit Expense Reports
- Reconcile Transactions
- Access your Dashboard for Realtime View of your Cash Flow
- Use an additional app for Employees for Submitting Time Sheets, Request Time Off, and View Paystubs

One thing that sets Xero apart from other software is that it also has the capability to have a developer design and customize your own app by providing the API to allow for integration to your Xero account.

There is also a 24/7 customer support for those times that you have issues with your account, allowing you to have your books back up without losing the sale. However, there is one drawback to Xero. There are not many accountant and bookkeepers who know the software. Therefore, it brings in limitations to finding someone to keep your books.

Zoho Books

If you are a sole proprietor, freelancer or E-Commerce with a home-base business, then this is a great bookkeeping software for you. It is easy to use and affordable. It will allow you to connect with all your accounts and it covers all the basic needs of your business.

Zoho Books offer three pricing plans. The basic plan is $9 per month. This plan only supports one user and allows you to add 50 contacts. Other features include:

- Reconcile Transactions
- Create Invoices
- Track Expenses
- Manage Projects
- Manage Time Sheets

The standard plan is $19 per month and supports 2 users. It also allows for 500 contacts to be added. This plan includes:

- Reconcile Transactions
- Create Invoices
- Track Expenses
- Manage Projects
- Manage Time Sheets
- Track Bills
- Track Vendor Credits
- Add Reporting Tags to your Transactions

The professional plan is $29 per month and allows for 10 users. This plan also allows for unlimited contacts. It also includes:

- Reconcile Transactions
- Create Invoices
- Track Expenses
- Manage Projects
- Manage Time Sheets
- Track Bills

- Track Vendor Credits
- Add Reporting Tags to your Transactions
- Create Sales Orders
- Create Purchase Orders
- Manage Inventory

Zoho Books has one of the best customer services and support. The phones are open 24 hours a day, five days a week.

One disadvantage of Zoho Books is that it does not offer payroll services. If you have employees than you would need software that is for payroll. If you do not have employees then this is the best for you and your business.

FreshBooks

I mentioned earlier that there is software for bookkeeping that is great for those who want more accessibility through mobile apps. What makes FreshBooks the best is that you can find almost all the features in the mobile app that you have on the website. Keep in mind, if your business has inventory then this may not be the software for you.

Most all the software we have been talking about is based on features. With FreshBooks, the pricing is based on active clients. For the Lite plan, it is $15 per month and allows you to bill up to five clients. The plus plan is $25 per month and allows you to bill up 50 clients. The premium plan is $50 and allows to bill up to 500 clients.

For each of the plans you can add contractors at no additional cost. However, if you need to add employees it is an extra $10 per month for each employee. Contractors and employees can view different parts of the books.

Employees can:

- View and Create Invoices and Expenses
- View the Dashboard
- Generate Reports
- Contractors can:
- View Projects they have been Assigned to
- Track Time towards the Assigned Projects
- Create and Send You Invoices for their Time

FreshBooks also has some timesaving features. You can create, send and manage invoices easily. This can be done from your computer or mobile app. It also allows for faster payments and makes tracking your expenses easy and allows for project management and time tracking.

With all software, customer service is a must. You will find both phone and email support. However, it is not 24/7 support. They do have hours between 8 a.m. to 8 p.m. eastern standard time Monday through Friday. With such great interface of mobile app then they also have support for those issues that may arise as well.

Wave Accounting

That brings us to the last bookkeeping software we are going to look at, Wave Accounting. Wave Accounting is great if you do not have much equity to start with, as this software is free. Yes, that's right, I did say free.

Wave Accounting is designed for very small businesses with 10 employees or fewer and no inventory. If your business offers services, then you may want to try it out. If you plan on growing your business, eventually you will need to transition to another form of software.

Keep in mind, what keeps Wave Accounting free is the use of advertising. That means it will not only post advertising on the software while you use it, but it will also include its branding on your communications with customers.

You can also add credit card processing for small fee per transaction. The same goes for payroll processing as this can be added for $15 per month as well as an additional $4 per employee per month.

Keep in mind, Wave Accounting does still offer the basics for the needs of your company. With the advertising, if you want to have your business separated from all the ads, then you may want chose a different software such as Zoho Books.

Create a Logo

One thing that will set your business apart from the rest is the business logo you create. This logo will be displayed on invoices, business cards, brochures, website, etc.

This should represent your business. You do not need to spend a lot of money on a good design. Search around and you will find a lot of sites that offer logo design for cheaper.

If you have some creative talent and want to create your own you can do that as well. A great place to start is through https://www.canva.com. This site is user friendly and free, although you do not need to use this site. You can easily create it in Word, Photoshop, Paint, etc. Make sure to save your logo as a JPG or PNG. If you use Word, then hit print screen and copy it into Paint so that you can save it in the proper format. Chose a good size for the logo and crop if needed. You may want to save different sizes as well. For example, you may have one size for your invoices, a size for your business cards, and a size for your letterhead when sending out emails and letters on behalf of the business.

Monthly Bookkeeping Reports

Many times, businesses start to struggle because they do not know how the business is doing from the beginning. A good rule of thumb is to actively have the books up-to-date and always accurate. This will help when you do reports.

Also, make sure you are pulling the reports monthly. Do not just wait until the end of the quarter or year. If you have the reports each month it will give you a better understanding of how your business is doing and can help you make changes, if needed, for the following month.

With that said, I also want you to understand it is also just as important to do quarterly and yearly reports. This will help you judge how the business is doing overall throughout the year and throughout the years.

Hire Employees

Adding employees to your business is not always the easiest to keep up with. It brings new responsibilities as you will need to keep track and pay their wages. One thing that can help with this is the bookkeeping software applications that we have discussed. It is worth ensuring you have the payroll feature if you have employees. Your employees rely on this paycheck.

Granted with payroll, you also have payroll taxes. This money belongs to the government. One thing that could help with this is to have a separate savings account within your business account for holding all the payroll taxes. That way when it comes time to pay the government the money is already set aside.

Make sure you are filing the correct documents for payroll on time otherwise you could encounter added fines.

Try New Systems

There are so many systems out there that will help your business succeed. We have talked about a few of the software programs used for bookkeeping. However, if you add too many systems at once it could be overwhelming for you, your employees, and your customers.

As the business owner, you need to carefully select the applications you need for your business. A good rule of thumb is only try the systems that are needed for either maintenance or growth. If your business does not need it for either one of these, then do not add them! One thing that could help with this is having a website or mobile app designed that integrates everything you need for your business. You can add a feature that allows you, your employees, and your customers to access the same app, but based on their credentials they will only have access to what is needed for them.

Keep in mind, if you introduce one system at a time you will be able to give everyone a chance to learn the system before introducing the next.

Be Hands-On with your Bookkeeper

As a business owner, you need to take a hands-on approach with your bookkeeper. In the starting phase, you might not afford to hire a bookkeeper and therefore must do it yourself or have one of your staff members do it. Always make sure you know what is going on with your accounts if you allow your staff to do the bookkeeping.

Bookkeeping is basic transactions, but you do need to see those reports each month, quarter, and year. If you record an invoice or expense in the wrong account the books can still balance but the accounts may not.

A bookkeeper needs to know and understand where all transactions will be recorded. I would also say the same about the business owner. If you are the business owner, you need to read the reports each month and know if something does not look right and needs to be reviewed. The same goes with the bookkeeper. If you are the bookkeeper, you need to go through all the transactions that were recorded that month to ensure that they were recorded in the correct account before the reports are generated.

One thing you could do is have a professional consultant bookkeeper look at the books for any errors. If you are worried about upsetting your bookkeeper, then add it to your company policy that a routine audit will be conducted at the end of each month or quarter.

Outsource to a Bookkeeper

If you, as the business owner, is also the bookkeeper for an extended period of time, then you may want to outsource your bookkeeping. This can be the most cost effective as you are only paying for a couple hours of work. On the other hand, if you had an employee assigned to it, you are paying a monthly wage. You can also outsource to ensure that the books are being handled by a professional and will be accurate.

In general, it could take a professional bookkeeper only two to four hours to process an entire month of transactions and provide your business the monthly reports you require.

If you feel that you can handle some of the bookkeeping and only want the professional to handle specific areas you can do that as well.

One of the benefits of outsourcing to a professional is that they can give great business advice that will help your business grow. Some of this advice could be, but is not limited to:

- New software and if they would be a good fit for your business
- Attend business meetings with you and your banker

- Help with annual budget and cashflow reports
- Train office employees

Chapter 3 – Managing Assets, Liabilities and Owner's Equity

Before we start to break down the financial reports, let's consider the management of the three areas of the accounting equations. Those are assets, liabilities, and owner's equity.

Assets

Here are some assets to be aware of:

- The Credit and Debit Cards the Business Holds
- Loans that your company has made to others
- Money Market Accounts
- Brokerage Services
- Equipment
- Fixed Income
- Real Estate or Property
- Commodities and International Investments

Many businesses will need some kind of funding. Therefore, when selecting a financial institution, you should know what the bank is looking at when deciding upon who to give a loan.

The following is a list of what most banks look for:

- Minimum Years in Business
- Minimum Revenue

- Minimum FICO Score: Does the loan require personal credit?
- Profitability: Does the loan require you to bring in a profit?
- Bankruptcy: Even if you have filed for bankruptcy, do you still qualify?
- Credit Card Volume: Some loans rely on credit card volume used by your business. This is because those loans are paid off based on the volume.
- Accounts Receivable: Some alternative loans will consider your accounts receivable in their decision.
- Existing Debt: Do you have a debt with another lender? If so, check to see what they require if you take out another loan.

A Small Business Administration Loan:

Years in Business Required	2+ years
Revenue	$50,000
Credit Score	640+
Profitability Required	No
Bankruptcy Allowed	Yes! You could qualify with no less than 3 years after filing for bankruptcy.
Credit Card Volume Factored	No
Accounts Receivable Factored	No
Second Position Allowed for Debt	No! The SBA will not take a second position to another lender.

Short-Term Loan:

Years in Business Required	6+ months
Revenue	$65,000+
Credit Score	500+
Profitability Required	No
Bankruptcy Allowed	Yes! You could qualify with no less than 1 year after filing for bankruptcy.
Credit Card Volume Factored	In some cases. If it is, there is a minimum of $3,000+

Accounts Receivable Factored	No
Second Position Allowed for Debt	In some cases

Medium-Term Loan:

Years in Business Required	1+ year
Revenue	$150,000+ in most cases. Sometimes if only 1 lender they will consider $25,000+
Credit Score	600+
Profitability Required	No
Bankruptcy Allowed	Yes! You could qualify with no less than 2 years after filing for bankruptcy.
Credit Card Volume Factored	No
Accounts Receivable Factored	No
Second Position Allowed for Debt	In some cases

Line of Credit:

Years in Business Required	1+ year
Revenue	$200,000+
Credit Score	600+
Profitability Required	Yes
Bankruptcy Allowed	Yes! You could qualify with no less than 2 years after filing for bankruptcy.
Credit Card Volume Factored	No
Accounts Receivable Factored	Yes
Second Position Allowed for Debt	In some cases

Invoice Financing:

Years in Business Required	6+ months
Revenue	$50,000+

Credit Score	500+
Profitability Required	No
Bankruptcy Allowed	Yes
Credit Card Volume Factored	No
Accounts Receivable Factored	Yes
Second Position Allowed for Debt	Yes

Startup Loan:

Years in Business Required	0+
Revenue	0+
Credit Score	700+
Profitability Required	No
Bankruptcy Allowed	Yes! You could qualify with no less than 3 year after filing for bankruptcy.
Credit Card Volume Factored	No
Accounts Receivable Factored	No
Second Position Allowed for Debt	No

Liability

We also need to look at the liabilities of the company. These can include things like customer deposits, fund securities, etc. It can be good to keep contact with a good financial advisor that can either handle or help you handle the assets and liabilities.

Although, most people who are just starting out cannot afford a financial advisor. No matter how good you are in business and keeping your business in control you will have some sort of liability.

However, you can ensure that your business and assets are protected from these liabilities that can arise.

We will briefly discuss how we can protect ourselves.

Personal Liability:

Even though you incorporate or form a Limited Liability Company you may have personal liabilities. These are some circumstances that would be a personal liability:

- Person guarantee a loan for the business
- Your actions result in an injury
- You committed a crime or operated your business illegally
- You do not operate your business as if it's separate from your personal accounts.

Business Liability Insurance:

To better help you protect yourself it is a very good idea to have business liability insurance. This will protect your small business from personal injury or property damage if a lawsuit arises. Here are the three types of business liability insurance:

- General Liability Insurance: Protects from injury claims, property damages, and claims of negligence and advertising claims.
- Product Liability Insurance: Protects against financial loss as a result of defective products that cause harm.
- Professional Liability Insurance: Protects business owners who provide a service. Protects against malpractice, errors, negligence, and omissions.

Owner's Equity

There really is not a set way to manage the owner's equity. This is based off the investments from stocks, the money you put into the company, and the amount you withdraw from the company. For these types of transactions, you can use a regular business bank account and link it to your bookkeeping software.

Chapter 4 – Using Ledgers and Journals to Track Business Activity

Before we can start to understand the financial reports, we need to look at where the information comes from. We can start with the journal entries that are made by the business and when those entries are posted to the ledgers. Next, we will then look at how we can track those transactions. Knowing where the transactions came from and where they are listed in the financial reports will help you better understand the reports that are created.

Financial Journals

Most of the time when we talk about journaling in accounting and bookkeeping we refer to the General Journal.

How many times have you looked at the General Journal and gotten lost on how the business is really doing? Don't worry! If you said a lot or all the time then you are not alone. That is why in bookkeeping, along with the General Journal, you have six additional journals. They are:

1. Cash Receipts Journal (CRJ)
2. Cash Payments Journal (CPJ)
3. Sales Journal (SJ)
4. Sales Returns Journal (SRJ)
5. Purchase Journal (PJ)
6. Purchase Returns Journal (PRJ)
7. General Journal (GJ)

Let's look at each of the seven journals to get a better understanding. In the examples, you will also see the ref field. There may be references there that do not correspond to a journal. That is because they will correspond to a specific ledger. We will be talking about ledgers later in this chapter.

Remember, if you are using accounting software then all this is done for you through that software. However, it is nice to know the basics so that you can better understand where the financial reports are coming from.

Cash Receipts Journal (CRJ)

When you receive cash, you will record it in the Cash Receipts Journal. The categories of the CRJ are:

- Date
- Details
- Ref.
- Bank
- Income
- Debtors
- Sundry

When you look at the CRJ, you will see three major categories: The bank is the total of each line and shows how much cash was received. Income is taken from receipts where you brought in money, while debtors is when you have a receipt where you paid out money. The category "sundry" is a word that means "various," miscellaneous," or "general."

Here is an example of a CRJ:

DATE	DETAILS	REF	BANK	INCOME	DEBTORS	SUNDRY
1	Capital	S1	15,000	-	-	15,000
7	Loan	S2	5,000	-	-	5,000
12	Service rendered	L1	10,500	10,500	-	-
30	Smiths	L2	5,000	-	5,000	-
Total			35,500	10,500	5,000	20,000

Cash Payments Journal (CPJ)

Much like the CRJ, the Cash Payments Journal shows where the cash has been paid out of the business. The categories of the CPJ are:

- Date
- Details
- Ref.
- Expenses
- Creditors
- Sundry
- Bank

If you notice, the categories are the same except for income is now expenses, the Debtors is now Creditors, and the bank category is now at the end. Here is an example of a CPJ:

DATE	DETAILS	REF	EXPENSES	CREDITORS	SUNDRY	BANK
8	Equipment purchased	A1	-	-	12,000	12,000
9	Drawings	S3	-	-	500	500
12	Salary	E1	4,000	-	-	4,000
13	Telephone company	L2	-	200	-	200
15	Loan repayment	S4	-	-	4,000	4,000
Totals			4,000	200	16,500	20,700

Keep in mind that if you prefer using a cash book, it is a combination of the SRJ and the SPJ. This will allow for the cash book to show all receipts and payments together.

If your business has a petty cash fund, you can keep track of this fund with additional journals and use the same format as the CRJ and the CPJ.

Sales Journal (SJ)

Whether you're are offering services, merchandise, or both, I think we can agree that sales are important. That's why a Sales Journal is a great tool to have. Remember that only the income on credit will be recorded in the SJ. Once it is paid and your business receives cash for the service, then it will be recorded in the cash receipts journal.

The categories for the SJ:

- Date
- Debtor
- Ref.
- Services rendered

Here is an example of what a Sales Journal may look like:

DATE	DEBTOR	REF	SERVICE RENDERED
8	Smiths	L2	5,000
Total			5,000

Sales Returns Journal (SRL)

If you have a company that has merchandise, you occasionally deal with returned merchandise. You will use the Sales Returns Journal to track the returns that have been originally sold.

The categories within the SRL are:

- Date
- Debtor
- Ref.
- Sales returns

Here is an example of what an SRL may look like:

DATE	DEBTOR	REF	SALES RETURNS
16	J. Jacobs	R1	300

Total			300

Purchases Journal (PJ)

When your business has inventory, you will also have a Purchases Journal. This journal is used when your business purchases inventory on credit. Remember, a PJ only applies to inventory. Therefore, not all assets are recorded here. Only inventory purchased on credit will be recorded in the PJ.

The categories on a Purchases Journal are:

- Date
- Creditor
- Ref.
- Purchases

Here is what a Purchases Journal may look like:

DATE	CREDITOR	REF	PURCHASES
3	J.P. Manufacturers	P1	5,500
5	Wood Importers Inc.	P2	1,500
Total			7,000

Purchases Returns Journal (PRJ)

Just like the SRJ, the Purchases Returns Journal is for recording merchandise that your business purchased on credit and then needed to return to the merchandise.

The categories for the PRJ are:

- Date
- Creditor
- Ref.
- Purchases returns

Here is an example of what a Purchases Returns Journal may look like:

DATE	CREDITOR	REF	PURCHASES RETURNS
3	J.P. Manufacturers	P1	100
5	Wood Importers Inc.	P2	1,500
Total			1,600

General Journal (GJ)

So many times, we talk about the General Journal as it holds all the transaction a business makes. When you think about it, by using that definition of a general journal you are referring to all seven journals. However, the General Ledger does that very thing. That is right! The General Journal has all the transactions that do not fit into the other six journals.

The format is simple. It includes:

- Date
- Description
- Ref.
- Debit
- Credit

Here is an example of what a basic journal may look like:

DATE	DISCRIPTION	REF	DEBIT	CREDIT
Apr 2	Description for the Debit		1,000	
	Indent the description for the Credit(s)			1,000
16	Description for the Debit		7,000	
	Indent the description for the Credit(s)			7,000
19	Description for the Debit		3,000	
	Indent the description for the			3,000

	Credit(s)			
Totals			11,000	11,000

When working with the general journal, always remember the Debits and Credits must equal.

The Ledgers

For bookkeeping and double-entry accounting there are three main categories of ledgers we need to look at.

1. General Ledger (GL)
2. Accounts Receivable Ledger (ARL)
3. Accounts Payable Ledger (APL)

You may think that it is a waste of time to record the entries twice. You will find that just because you have journaled the transactions in one of the seven journals it is beneficial to organize the transactions into the ledger accounts as well.

General Ledger (GL)

When you set up your business bookkeeping, a Chart of Accounts was created. Each account on this Chart of Accounts has a Ref number assigned to it. This reference comes in handy for both the Journals and the Ledgers. For each account on the Chart of Accounts you will have a General Ledger for the account. In each General Ledger, you will have either a Debit or Credit normal balance.

In the seven journals, you would record the ledger or associated journal in the ref field. In the ledgers, you will record the corresponding journal in the ref field.

Let's look at the General Journal for your business's Cash account.

Account: Cash - Ref: 100

DATE	DESCRIPTION	REF	DEBIT	CREDIT
Apr 1	Opening Balance		4,500	
1		J1		25.00
4		J1	180.00	
4		J1		250.00
8		J2		145.00

10		J2	25.00	
Total	Note: End of Month totals)		4,285	

The total is calculated at the end of each month and carried forward to the next month as the new opening balance. There will be a ledger for each account on the Chart of Accounts.

Accounts Receivable Ledger (ARL) and Accounts Payable Ledger (APL)

The Accounts Receivable and Accounts Payable Ledgers are subsidiary ledger accounts. These are accounts that are in addition to the General Ledgers but are mainly for tracking the receivables and payables.

You may have multiple accounts of vendors who owe you money or you owe money too. Each account will have their own ledger.

Accounts Receivable will have a Debit normal balance while Accounts Payable will have a Credit normal balance.

Here is an example of each type of ledger:

Debtor: A. Franklin - Ref: AR-F

DATE		REF	DEBIT	CREDIT	BALANCE
July 18	Terms 60 days	SJ1	150.00		150.00
27	Terms 30 days	SJ1	190.00		340.00

Creditor: Smiths Manufacturer   Ref: AP-S

DATE		REF	DEBIT	CREDIT	BALANCE
July 14	Terms 60 days	SJ1		60.00	60.00
21	Terms 30 days	SJ1		100.00	160.00

Tracking Transactions

Now that we have the journals and the ledgers, how do we track all the activity that is going on? It is simple. Look at the Ref column. The Ref column will show the link between the seven journals and the ledgers from the Chart of Accounts.

In addition to the journals and ledgers, you will note that the income statement (profit and loss statement) and the balance sheet will be constructed from the General Ledgers.

Chapter 5 – Employees

Whenever you bring on new employees there are certain things that you need to look at. This is the basics of your payroll structure that is created for the business.

Now what is the plan? How are you going to gather what is needed for each new employee? Here are 10 steps that will help you establish this goal. We will talk about each step so you can successfully hire new employees.

1. Get an Employer Identification Number (EIN).
2. Find out whether you need state or local tax IDs.
3. Decide if you want an independent contractor or an employee.
4. Ensure new employees return a completed W-4 form.
5. Schedule pay periods to coordinate tax withholding for IRS.
6. Create a compensation plan for holiday, vacation and leave.
7. Choose an in-house or external service for administration payroll
8. Decide who will manage your payroll system.
9. Know which records must stay on file and for how long.
10. Report payroll taxes as needed on a quarterly and annual basis.

Filing and withholding taxes may seem stressful. It does not need to be. In fact, the IRS maintains an Employer's Tax Guide. This can be found on the IRS website at www.irs.gov. Search for Publication 15 (2017), (Circular E), Employer's Tax Guide.

Get an Employer Identification Number (EIN)

If your business is about to hire employees as it is expanding, then you will need an Employer Identification Number (EIN). This number is a nine-digit number and will look like this: 12-3456789. It will be used for identifying the tax account of the employer. There are certain types of businesses that need an EIN who do not have employees. For this you can research the Employer's Tax Guide to find out if you need one or not.

There are two ways to apply for an EIN. The quickest is to apply through the IRS website at IRS.gov/ein. It will give you instructions and allow you to fill out the application electronically. The second is to fill out form SS-4, also found on the IRS website and fax or mail it to IRS. For both methods, be sure you have all the required information you need for the application. The best way is to find form SS-4 and fill that out before you fill out the online application. This way you have all the required information and can easily fill out the online application. Keep in mind, you will need to fill out the online application in one setting and it times out after 15 minutes of inactivity.

On the occasion that you bought someone's business, you will still need to file for your own EIN. This number is unique to the employer.

When it comes time to file your return and you do not have the EIN yet, file a paper return and write "Applied for 20 April 20XX" in the space shown for the number. Keep in mind, the date is the date you applied for the EIN.

All states have federal taxes that will need to be withheld. Your EIN is also known as your Federal Tax ID. A good rule of thumb is to apply for one as soon as you register your business.

Find out whether you need state or local tax IDs

Your state may not require you to pay state taxes. There are seven states that do not have income taxes and an additional two who only impose tax if the income is from dividends.

The best way to know if you need a state tax ID is by visiting your states website.

Decide if you want an independent contractor or an employee

A good question is if you are going to hire an independent contractor or an employee. This could determine how the taxes are withheld from the payroll.

Contractors will be operating under a different business name and will invoice you for the work. Keep in mind, there are times where a contractor can qualify as an employee in a legal sense. If you choose to hire contractors, you should get familiar with the Equal Employment Opportunity Commission Guide and the Fair Labor Standards Act.

Ensure new employees return a completed W-4 form

Every employee must have a current W-4 on file with your business. This is needed so you can accurately dedicate taxes for your employees. So, make sure that each new employee files the W-4 with your business as part of the hiring process. The form can be found either on the IRS website or by Google searching for W-4.

1. The lines that need to be filled out are:
2. First and Last Name, Home Address, City, Stat, and ZIP
3. Social Security Number
4. Single, Married, or Married but withhold at higher single rate
5. Check if name is different than SS Card
6. Total number of Allowances
7. Additional amount to be withheld
8. Claim exemptions

The employee will sign and date the form. Line eight is for the employer and will include employer's name and address, office code, and EIN.

Schedule pay periods to coordinate tax withholding for IRS

Most of us have worked for someone and you should have noticed that they had a set pay period. This makes it easy for your employees to know when they will be getting paid. Many employers have the pay period as every two weeks, while others, such as the military, have it on specific days. For instance, the military uses the 1st and the 15th of the month to pay their soldiers.

No matter what schedule you use, be consistent. Keep the same schedule for all employees and do not change it.

Create a compensation plan for holidays, vacation and leave

There are many different plans that you need to consider now that you are going to have employees. Now, we are going to look at the compensation plan.

Does your business work on holidays? If so how are you going to pay your employees and how long will they work? When your employees work holidays, you need to pay those employees 1.5 per hour, also known as time and a half. Let's say the hourly rate is $10 and they worked 6 hours on a holiday that qualifies for holiday pay. They will get $60 for their shift plus $30 for the holiday. Therefore, for 6 hours on a holiday at $10 per hour you will pay your employee $90.

At the same time, if you offer vacation pay, sick pay, or emergency leave pay, then you will calculate that pay based off the hours they would have normally worked that day.

For the compensation plan you will withhold taxes like you normally would for their normal pay period.

Choose an in-house or external service for administrating payroll

Making the decision to have your payroll done in-house or outsourced to another business can be one of the biggest decisions you will make for your businesses payroll. Here are a few questions you can ask yourself to help you make the decision a little easier. After all, the wrong decision for the payroll could cost you a lot of money.

1. How much control do you want over the process of paying your employees?
2. How frequently do your employees get paid?
3. Do different groups of employees get paid at different times?
4. How often do you have to give out last minute pay checks and changes?
5. How often do you process off-cycle payments?
6. How complicated is your payroll? Do you have employee benefits and deductions, allowances, etc.?
7. Does your organization have the resources to support an in-house payroll?
8. Do you have someone on your team that has a good understanding of payroll and statutory reporting?
9. How many accounts do you need to update on the general ledger?
10. Do you want a record of all payroll transactions and changes made?

These are only a few questions you may want to consider. Keep in mind, the longer an outside source needs to work on it the more money you need to pay them. If you can limit it to only a few hours a week, then it would be good to use an outside source and utilize your employee in another area of the business. However, if you feel that it will cost you more to pay an outside source due to the number of transactions that need to be done and it turns into a fulltime job, you may want to consider doing the payroll in-house.

Decide who will manage your payroll system

Now that you have your payroll system set up, another big decision is deciding upon a manager for it. For a small business, you may want to outsource this work as it will not be much work in the beginning. As your business grows, it would be a good idea for you to have an employee or yourself, as the business owner, to get trained on good bookkeeping practices.

Know which records must stay on file and for how long

One problem that many small businesses face is the duration of keeping files. That is why I am adding it here. Some would suggest that you should keep tax information for the business forever. I would not advise this unless you have an iCloud service that meets the security requirements for safeguarding the business and employees' information. Besides, if you are a big company, that is a lot of storage space that you would need just for files.

The IRS can audit your tax records for 3 years and can extend that for 6 years.

- **Business Tax Returns:** Should be kept until IRS can no longer audit your tax returns. (6 years)

- **Payroll Tax Records:** This will include time sheets, wages, tax deposits, benefits and tips. (4 years of taxes are due or when you paid them. Whichever is the later date)

- **Current Employee Files:** (7 years after employee leaves business or 10 years if employee was involved in a work-related accident)

- **Job Application Information:** (3 years even if you do not hire the employee)

- **Ownership Records:** Includes business formation documents, annual meeting minutes. By-laws, stock-ledgers, and property deeds. Keep in mind, your business may not have all these documents. These documents will be anything you needed to form your business. (Retained Permanently)

- **Accounting Service Records:** This will include financial statements, check registers, profit and loss statements, budgets, general ledgers, cash books, and audit reports. (At minimum 7 years. I would recommend permanently as it will give you an outlook of how your business has grown.)

- **Operational Records:** This includes bank account statements, credit card statements, canceled checks, cash receipts, and check book stubs. (7 years)

I know it seems like a long time to hold onto these records. Keep in mind, you want to protect your business and keeping these records can safeguard your business when a problem may come up.

In today's world, everything is digital. You may want to invest in a server that meets the requirements needed to protect these files.

Report payroll taxes as needed on a quarterly and annual basis

Now that you have employees, you will need to report the payroll taxes. The taxes that must be deposited to the IRS are the federal income tax withholdings, social security, and Medicare taxes for both the employer and employee.

There are two deposit schedules. They are monthly and semi-monthly. Before you start each calendar year, look at the Publication 15 on the IRS website to determine which payment schedule you are required to use.

You have probably noticed I have referenced Publication 15 a few times. I would advise saving the publication as it has a lot of information you will be referring to while running your small business. Another one, depending on what form you are using, will be Publication 51.

Publication 15 will be for forms 941, 944, and 945. For form 943 you will use Publication 51.

As the employer, you will be required to report wages, tips, and other compensation paid by using the required forms. You will also report the taxes either by filing out the paper form and sending it into the IRS or by e-filing through the IRS website.

Let's look at the different forms:

Form 941 (Employer's Quarterly Federal Tax Form)

- Filed Quarterly
- Any employer who withholds federal income tax or social security and Medicare taxes

Form 943 (Employer's Annual Federal Tax Return for Agricultural Employees)

- Filed annually if reporting agricultural wages

Form 944 (Employer's Annual Federal Tax Return)

- Only if you have received a written notice about the 944 programs

Form 945 (Annual Return of Withheld Federal Income Tax)

- Only if you are filing to report backup withholdings

Form 940 (Employer's Annual Federal Unemployment (FUTA) Tax Return

- Only if you pay FUTA tax

With state taxes, they will vary from state to state. Check with your local business administration for small businesses for more details with the state tax reporting.

With all this talk about filing the taxes throughout the year, we should also mention the taxes when filing at the end of the year and what needs to get done at that time. Every business who has employees will need to prepare W2's. Because there is so much to cover for filing taxes and getting your business ready at the end of the year, I added a special bonus chapter at the end. This chapter will be dedicated to you and your bookkeeper to prepare your business for tax season.

Setting-Up Direct Deposit

Setting up direct deposit can be easy with the right tools. Many software programs have the feature to set up direct deposit. The nice thing is when you run your payroll and have your business bank account linked to the software, it will make it easier to get the payroll out each pay period.

You will need to get some basic information from the employee. Most banks will give them a form with all that information on it. Here is the basics of what you will need:

- Bank's Routing Number or ABA. It is a nine-digit number that is associated with the bank. Can be found on checks and the bank website.
- Checking / Savings Accounting Number
- Bank name and Address

There can be some cost to direct depositing the pay check. Some banks charge a transaction fee and per-check fee. Be prepared to handle this out of the business funds so that your employee gets what they earned.

Employee Benefits

The benefits that you can offer your employees are what will entice them to stay with your business. There are some benefits that you are required to offer by law. However, there are many that are optional.

Required Benefits

Let's look at the benefits you will be required to have:

- Social Security Taxes: All employers must pay the same rate of SS tax as the employees.
- Workers' Compensation: These are required through a commercial carrier, self-insured basis, or the State Workers' Compensation Program.
- Disability Insurance: Disability pay is required in in some states but not all. Check with your state if it is required.
- Leave benefits: Most leave benefits are optional. However, consult the Family and Medical Leave Act (FMLA) for those leave options that are required.
- Unemployment insurance: This varies from state to state. You may need to register with your state workforce agency.

Optional Benefits

There are many optional benefits that you may want to consider. A big one is a retirement plan. Even though medical insurance is not required, you can offer different types of medical plans. This will allow your employee to get better coverage based on their needs.

Incentive Programs

Offering incentive programs is another great way to reward your employees. Be creative and come up with some ways that would benefit your employees. Some ideas would be wellness programs, memberships, bonuses, discounts, etc.

If you are wanting to add incentives, make sure you add them to your employee's handbook. This way everyone knows what your business is offering. For accounting and bookkeeping purposes, you may want to consider a benefits administration software. This will make it easier when it comes time to keep the books.

Federal and State Labor Laws

The labor laws are very important, especially when it comes to hiring. There are specific guidelines when hiring veterans, foreign workers, household employees, child labor, and people with disabilities. This is only to name a few as there are many others.

For complete details about these different labor laws, consult the Department of Labor's federal and state law resources.

Chapter 6 – Depreciation

Your small business may buy equipment that is supposed to last several years. However, over those years your equipment will lose some of its value.

For example, you buy a computer with Windows 7 for $575. Three years later your computer starts to break and you need to find parts. Over that time your depreciation went from $575 to about $50. At the same time, with as fast as technology is advancing you can no longer get parts. Now your depreciation of $50 is considered a recycling fee.

As you can see, over time your equipment will lose its value, and we need to calculate this into the bookkeeping. The depreciation can be an annual income tax deduction. It will be listed as an expense on the income statement. You can take advantage of this deduction by filing Form 4562 with your tax return. For more information about the Depreciation and requirements you must have, refer to Publication 946 (How to Depreciate Property).

For you to be able to claim a depreciation deduction there are a few guidelines that your property needs to meet.

- You must own the property. However, you can also depreciate capital improvements for property that you lease.

- The property must be used for business or to produce income. If you use the property for both business and personal you cannot deduct the property based on only business use of the property.

- The property must have a determined life span of more than one year.

However, even if you meet all the requirements of property deduction; you cannot deduct the following property:

- Any property that is placed in service and disposed the same year.

- Any equipment that is used to build capital improvements. You can add allowable depreciation on the equipment during the construction based on improvements.
- Certain term interests.

Most property can be depreciated. You can depreciate buildings, machinery, vehicles, furniture, and equipment. However, land cannot be depreciated. This is because you are expected to use the land for the lifetime of your business and it will never depreciate. However, the building on the land you operate your business from can be depreciated.

You will need to identify many items when filing taxes and using Form 4562 for the depreciation deduction. This is to ensure the proper depreciation of the property. These items include:

- Depreciation method for the property
- Class life of the asset
- Whether the property is "Listed Property"
- Whether you elect to expense any portion of the asset
- Whether you qualify for any "bonus" first year depreciation
- Depreciable basis of the property

How do we calculate depreciation? There are two different methods which we will discuss now: Book Depreciation and the Tax Depreciation.

Book Depreciation

For the books, you will often hear of the book depreciation. This type is mainly for accounting and bookkeeping purposes. The goal for this type of depreciation is to match the cost of an asset with the revenue it earns over the period of its lifetime. The most common method for this type of depreciation is the straight-line method. This can be calculated in two ways.

- Annual Depreciation = (COST – Residual Value) / Useful Life
- Annual Depreciation = (COST – Residual Value) * Rate of depreciation

Let's look at each area so you will be familiar with the different terms.

- Cost: Original cost of the property or equipment.
- Residual Value: This is also known as the scrap value. What will be the value of the property or equipment at the end of its life-spam?
- Useful Life: This is the amount of time you plan on keeping and using the equipment before you dispose of it.

- Rate of depreciation: This is the percentage of the useful life-span that is used in an accounting period. This can be calculated as follows:

Rate of depreciation = 1 / Useful Life * 100%

Tax Depreciation

There are many methods that you can use to calculate depreciation. Therefore, you do not need to stick to only one type. When it comes to taxes, the IRS likes the accelerated depreciation method the best. This method returns more of your money early in the asset's life. There are a few different methods you can use to get an accelerated depreciation.

- Declining Balance Depreciation = Rate * Net Book Value

For this formula let's look at what rate a book value are.

- Rate: This is a fixed rate and can be calculated as: (salvage Value / Cost)(1 / Years)
- Net Book Value: Original cost – accumulated depreciation to date on the asset

We also need to look at the double declining balance.

- Double Declining Rate = 2 / Useful Life
- Double Declining Balance Depreciation = Net Book Value * 2 / Useful life

With depreciation, make sure you keep your receipts. This will help your bookkeeper, accountant, and auditors check to make sure there are no mistakes before tax time and each month.

Chapter 7 – Adjusting Entries

You will find that adjusting entries are very important for your small business. These are journal entries that turn your accounting records into accrual based accounting. Normally these entries are made prior to issuing the financial statements.

Many times, adjusting entries are for expenses. However, there are times that an adjusting entry is needed for revenue.

There are two scenarios that need an adjusting entry before the financial statements are issued.

- When nothing has been inputted into the accounting records for certain expenses or revenue, although those expenses or revenue did occur and need to be included in the current income statement and balance sheet for that period.

- When there has been an entry into the records, but the amount will need to be divided up between more than one accounting period.

Asset Accounts

When you make adjusting entries, you assure that both the balance sheet and income statement are in check. This means that they need to be up-to-date based on the accrual basis of accounting.

A good way to begin is by examining and reviewing each balance on the balance sheet. Let's look at the following example and break it down. This will be based on the account balances before any adjustments are made.

The areas that we will be focusing on are the following:

- Cash - $1,800

- Accounts Receivable - $4,600

- Allowance for Doubtful Accounts - $0
- Supplies - $1,100
- Prepaid Insurance - $1,500
- Equipment - $25,000
- Accumulated Depreciation-Equipment - $7,500

Joe's Parcel Services

Preliminary Balance Sheet-before adjusting entries

December 31, 2015

ASSETS		LIABILITIES	
Cash	$ 1,800	Notes payable	$ 5,000
Accounts receivable	4,600	Accounts payable	2,500
Supplies	1,100	Wages payable	1,200
Prepaid insurance	1,500	Unearned revenues	1,300
Equipment	25,000	Total liabilities	10,000
Accumulated dereciation	(7,500)		
		OWNER'S EQUITY	
		Joe John, Captial	16,500
Totl assets	$ 26,500	Total liabilities & Owner's Equity	$ 26,500

Cash - $1,800

In the general ledger, the cash account has a balance of $1,800. However, before creating the balance sheet, I want you to ask yourself two questions.

1. Is $1,800 the true amount of cash?

2. Does it agree with what was figured based on the bank reconciliation?

In the case of our example the amount $1,800 is correct. However, if cash does not match with the bank reconciliation, adjustments will be needed to bring the balance sheet in check. Examples of this would be service charges, banking fees, and check printing charges. These entries would need to be entered into the cash account to ensure that it matches the bank statements.

Accounts Receivable - $4,600

For this account, you may want to review any unpaid invoices. They are often found in the accounts receivable subsidiary ledger. For this we will assume that $4,600 is accurate for the amounts not yet paid.

The balance sheet needs to report all amounts. This is to include the money not yet paid but due to the business. The same goes for all revenue that has been billed.

After careful review, we learned that $3,000 of services has been earned. This is dated as of December 31, although it will not be billed until January 10. In order to have that information on the December financial statements, you need to make an adjusting entry.

Remember, all entries will have at least a credit and a debit. The two accounts that are affected will be Accounts Receivable and Service Revenue. Accounts Receivable has a normal debit balance and is part of the balance sheet accounts. Service Revenues has a normal credit balance and is part of the income statement accounts.

The adjusting entry will look like this:

Date	Account Name	Debit	Credit
Dec 31 2015	Accounts Receivable	3,000	
	Service Revenues		3,000

When we look at the previous balance of $4,600 for accounts receivable and then make the adjusting entry of $3,000, the new balance for this account will be $7,600.

Allowance for Doubtful Accounts - $0

If you notice, this account is not listed on the balance sheet. That is because it has a $0 balance. It is common for accounts with a $0 balance to not appear on the balance sheet.

At one point your business may have accounts that are not collected for varies reasons. Instead of reducing the Accounts Receivable by issuing a credit on the ledgers you will report it in the Allowance for Doubtful Accounts.

Therefore, let's say $600 will not be collected. That means that $600 needs to be reported in the Allowance for Doubtful Account. There will be two accounts involved for this transaction. You will have Allowance for Doubtful Accounts found on the balance sheet. This account has a credit normal balance. The other account will be Bad Debts Expense found on the income statement. This account will have a normal debit balance.

The adjusting entry for this will be:

Date	Account Name	Debit	Credit
Dec 31 2015	Bad Debts Expense	600	
	Allowance for Doubtful Accounts		600

This transaction will give the Allowance for Doubtful Account a balance of $600.

As you go through the balance sheet, keep in mind which accounts will be affected and which accounts that are affected and whether they have a normal debit or credit.

You should take the time to see if you can figure out the remaining adjusting entries for the asset accounts. They are:

- Supplies - $1,100
    - Adjusting entry - $375 (Hint: The balance for supplies will be $725 and the accounts involved are Supplies and Supplies Expense)
- Prepaid Insurance - $1,500
    - Adjusting entry - $900 (Hint: The balance for Prepaid Insurance will be $600 and the accounts involved are Prepaid Insurance and Insurance Expense)
- Equipment - $25,000
    - No adjusting entry
- Accumulated Depreciation-Equipment - $7,500
    - Adjusting entry - $1,500 (Hint: The balance for Accumulated Depreciation-Equipment will be $9,000 and the accounts involved are Accumulated Depreciation-Equipment and Depreciation Expense-Equipment)

Adjusting Entries – Liability Accounts

As you review the accounts on the balance sheet, do not stop at the assets. The liability accounts need to be reviewed also. Check these accounts much the same way as the assets. See if you can record these transactions for the liability accounts.

- Notes Payable - $5,000
    - No adjusting entry needed
- Interest Payable - $0
    - Adjusting entry - $25 (Hint: The balance for the Interest Payable will be $25 and the accounts involved are Interest Payable and Interest Expense)
- Accounts Payable - $2,500

- Adjusting entry - $1,000 (Hint: The balance for Accounts Payable will be $3,500 and the accounts involved are Accounts Payable and Repairs & Maintenance Expense)
- Wages Payable - $1,200
  - Adjusting entry - $300 (Hint: The balance of Wages Payable will be $1,500 and the accounts involved are Wages Payable and Wages Expense)
- Unearned Revenues - $1,300
  - Adjusting entry - $800 (Hint: The balance for Unearned Revenues will be $500 and the accounts involved are Unearned Revenues and Service Revenues)

Keep in mind the normal balances for each account affected. Here is a list of all the accounts affected with their normal balances. As you do these adjusting entries and you do not know the normal balance for both transactions, figure out which one you do know. There will always be a debit and a credit for each transaction made. If it has a credit normal balance and the adjustment increases the account, then you will debit the other account.

- Accounts Receivable – Normal Debit Balance
- Service Revenues – Normal Credit Balance
- Allowance for Doubtful Accounts – Normal Credit Balance
- All Expenses – Normal Debit Balance
- Supplies – Normal Debit Balance
- Prepaid Insurance – Normal Debit Balance
- Accumulated Depreciation-Equipment – Normal Credit Balance
- Interest Payable – Normal Credit Balance
- Accounts Payable – Normal Credit Balance
- Wages Payable – Normal Credit Balance
- Unearned Revenues – Normal Credit Balance
- Service Revenues – Normal Credit Balance

Remember, all the accounts that will be affected for the adjusting entries will come from the balance sheet and the income statement.

Chapter 8 – Making Sense out of the Financial Statements

As a small business owner, you need to understand these basic statements so you will have a good outlook at where your business stands financially. This is where it is extremely important to communicate with your bookkeeper.

There are many financial statements that you could look at, depending on what you want to see. The basic statements we are going to look at are:

1. The Balance Sheet
2. The Income Statement
3. The Statement of Owner's Equity
4. The Statement of Cash Flow

These are also considered the BIG 4. The reason these are the big 4 is because they will give you a great understanding of where your business is financially. They are also the financial statements that investors use to make decisions and envision where your business could be in the future.

The Balance Sheet

The balance sheet is a good example of the accounting equation.

- Assets = Liabilities + Equity

Within this financial statement you will see the three areas divided up to show what accounts are listed under Assets, Liabilities, and Owner's Equity. The owner's equity represents retained earnings for your business. You will see all accounts on the balance sheet that do not have a $0 balance. Generally, accounts with a $0 balance do not need to be displayed.

There are two types of formats that will be used for a balance sheet. You will have the vertical or horizontal formats. You saw a horizontal format in the previous chapter.

Most business prefer the vertical format. However, the horizontal format has a better understand of the accounting equation. Let's look at the example from the last chapter.

ASSETS		LIABILITIES	
Cash	$ 1,800	Notes payable	$ 5,000
Accounts receivable	4,600	Accounts payable	2,500
Supplies	1,100	Wages payable	1,200
Prepaid insurance	1,500	Unearned revenues	1,300
Equipment	25,000	Total liabilities	10,000
Accumulated dereciation	(7,500)		
		OWNER'S EQUITY	
		Joe John, Captial	16,500
Totl assets	$ 26,500	Total liabilities & Owner's Equity	$ 26,500

From this example, I want you to keep in mind the accounting equation: Assets = Liabilities + Owner's Equity. If you notice, the balance is split in two sections and these sections are put side-by-side. On one side you have the Assets of $26,500. On the other side you have the liabilities of $10,000 and the Owner's Equity of $16,500. Let's take the liabilities and the owner's equity. Add those together and you will get $26,500.

With that in mind, let's put the accounting equation into the balance sheet. Left side: $26,500 (Assets) = Right side: $10,000 (Liabilities) + $16,500 (Owner's Equity). Now to see it more clearly you will have Left Side: $26,500 (Assets) = Right Side $26,500 (Liabilities + Owner's Equity).

Now what does this mean for your business? Based on your business's assets, the business is balanced in its financial obligations. This is to include investments and retained earnings.

You can think of it this way. Assets are the means a business uses to operate. On the other hand, the liabilities and owner's equity are the two ways you support the assets.

Now that we have an understanding of the balance sheet, what about the accounts that are listed in each section? It is important to know what accounts are asset, liability, and owner's equity.

Current Assets

These assets will have a life span of less than one year. This means they can be converted into cash. They include:

- Cash and Cash Equivalents
    - Cash
    - U.S. Treasuries
- Accounts Receivable
    - Sort-Term obligations owed to the business by the clients
- Inventory
    - Raw materials

Non-Current Assets

These assets cannot be turned into cash as easily. They are expected to be turned into cash within one year or have a life span of more than a year. Depreciation is usually calculated on these assets. Examples of these assets are:

- Tangible Assets
    - Machinery
    - Computers
    - Buildings
    - Land
- Intangible Assets
    - Goodwill
    - Patents
    - Copyright

Liabilities

When you look at the liabilities you should consider this as the obligations a business owes to others. Just like assets, they can be both current and long-term.

- Current Liabilities
    - Paid within one year
    - Accounts Payable

- Long-Term Liabilities
    - Debts that are more than one year
    - Non-Debts that are more than one year

Owner's Equity

This is the money that is invested in the business. The retained earnings from the income statement will also be transferred into the owner's equity at the end of the fiscal year. The owner's equity shows the net worth of your business. Types of accounts listed in the owner's equity:

- Capital – Money invested or earned by the business
- Drawing – Money that is withdrawn from the business

The Income Statement

To a business owner the income statement may look scary. However, it does not need to be. The income statement takes a closer look at the revenue or sales and the expenses of the business. This is usually done on a quarterly and annually basis throughout the fiscal year.

You may hear terms such as profits, earnings, and income when talking about the income statement. Keep in mind, they all mean the same thing.

There are two basic formats that you will use, the multi-step and the single-step formats. Here are the steps for each format:

- Multi-Step Format
    - Net Sales
    - Cost of Sales
    - Gross Income*
    - Selling, General and Administrative Expenses (SG&A)
    - Operating Income*
    - Other Income & Expenses
    - Pretax Income*
    - Taxes
    - Net Income (after tax)*
- Single-Step Format
    - Net Sales
    - Materials and Production

- Marketing and Administrative
- Research and Development Expenses (R&D)
- Other Income & Expenses
- Pretax Income
- Taxes
- Net Income

In the multi-step format there are four measures of profitability (*). Here is an example of an income statement:

	2015	2016
Net Sales	1,500,000	2,000,000
Cost of Sales	(350,000)	(375,000)
Gross Income	1,150,000	1,625,000
Operating Expenses (SG&A)	(235,000)	(260,000)
Operating Income	915,000	1,365,000
Other Income (Expenses)	40,000	60,000
Extraordinary Gain (Loss)	-	(15.,000)
Interest Expense	(50,000)	(50,000)
Net Profit Before Taxes (Pretax Income)	905,000	1,360,000
Taxes	(300,000)	(475,000)
Net Income	605,000	885,000

Once you know how the income statement is formatted and what is involved, you can see that between 2015 and 2016, there was an increase in sales by 33%. At the same time, the cost of sales was reduced from 23% to 19% in sales. If you look further you can see other increases and decreases between the two years.

Statement of Owner's Equity

The Statement of Owner's Equity can be used as a separate statement or it can be included in the balance sheet and income statements. It is also known as a Statement of Retained Earnings. This statement will show the stands of your businesses earnings.

Many times you will see this more with corporations as they have shareholders and pay out dividends. However, it can be a useful tool for a small business to show your retained earnings and financial standings.

The main purpose for this statement is to release financial information to the public, so they can decide if they want to invest into your business. It will also help analyze the health of your business.

Here is an example of a Statement of Owner's Equity.

Alex Printing and Design

Statement of Owner's Equity

For the Year Ending December 31, 2015

Alex, Capital: $100,000

Add: Additional Contributions: $10,000

Net Income: $57,100

Total: $167,100

Less: Alex, Drawings: $20,000

Alex, Capital – Dec. 31, 2015: $147,100

Statement of Cash Flow

One thing that is important is the flow of cash in and out of the business. The Statement of Cash Flow provides you with those answers. However, it is split up into four parts.

1. **Operating Activities** – This converts items that are on the income statement from the accrual basis of accounting to cash.
2. **Investing Activities** – This reports purchases and sales from long-term investments, property, plant and equipment.
3. **Financing Activities** – This reports issuance and repurchases of company bonds and stock as well as payments of dividends.
4. **Supplemental Information** – This reports exchanges of significant items. These items did not involve cash and will report the amount of income taxes and interests that are paid.

What is usually listed in each section? Let's take a look:
1. Operating Activities
    a. Accounts Receivable

b. Inventory
   c. Supplies
   d. Prepaid Insurance
   e. Other Current Assets
   f. Notes Payable
   g. Accounts Payable
   h. Wages Payable
   i. Payroll Taxes Payable
   j. Interest Payable
   k. Income Taxes Payable
   l. Unearned Revenues
   m. Other Current Liabilities
2. Investing Activities
   a. Long-term Investments
   b. Land
   c. Buildings
   d. Equipment
   e. Furniture & Fixtures
   f. Vehicles
3. Financing Activities
   a. Notes Payable (generally due after one year)
   b. Bonds Payable
   c. Deferred Income Taxes
   d. Preferred Stock
   e. Paid-in Capital in Excess of Par-Preferred Stock
   f. Paid-in Capital from Treasury Stock
   g. Retained Earnings
   h. Treasury Stock
4. Supplemental Information

Here is an example of a Statement of Cash Flow.

Frank's Deal LLC

Statement of Cash Flows

For Month Ended July 31, 2017

Operating Activities

    Net Income: $100

    Add back: Depreciation expense: $20

    Add back: Loss on sale of equipment: $180

    Increase in Inventory: ($200)

    Increase in supplies: ($150)

        Cash provided (used) in operating activities: ($50)

Investing Activities

    Purchase of office equipment: ($1,100)

    Proceeds from sale of office equipment: $900

        Cash provided (used) or investing activities: ($200)

Financing Activities

    Investment by owner: $2,000

Net increase in cash: $1,750

Cash at the beginning of the year: $0

Cash at July 31, 2017: $1,750

Knowing these four main financial statements will give you all the information you need for your business. These are the tools it takes to know the health of your business and plan for the future.

We have only touched base on the main financial statements. However, there are so many other reports you have access to. The main forms will give you all the financial information you will need to do ratios to see what the outcome of the business is. You can also compare the current years to see how the business has done from year-to-year.

Chapter 9 – Taxes for Small Businesses

A huge part of bookkeeping is preparing the books for tax season. That is why, as a bonus, I am adding this chapter about taxes for small businesses.

If you are just starting, you may feel overwhelmed at tax time. You should not need to feel this way. As long as you keep your records up-to-date, it should be a breeze when it comes time for taxes.

I want to share this checklist with you. This is a list of items that you will need when it is time to file your taxes for the business.

Income

- Gross receipts from sales or services
- Sales records (for accrual based taxpayers)
- Returns and Allowances
- Business checking/savings account interest (1099-INT or statement)
- Other Income

Cost of Goods Sold (if applicable)

- Inventory
- Beginning inventory total dollar amount
- Inventory purchases
- Ending inventory total dollar amount
- Items removed for personal purposes

- Materials & Supplies

Expenses

- Advertising
- Phones (landlines, fax or cell phones related to business)
- Computer & internet expenses
- Transportation and travel expenses
    - Local transportation
        - Business trip (mileage) log
        - Contemporaneous log or receipts for public transportation, parking, and tolls
    - Travel away from home
        - Airfare or mileage/actual expense if drove
        - Hotel
        - Meals, tips
        - Taxi, tips
        - Internet connection (hotel, internet café, etc.)
        - Other
- Commissions paid to subcontractors
    - File Form 1099-INT-MISCand 1096 as necessary
- Depreciation
    - Cost and first date of business use of asset
    - Records related to personal use of assets
    - Sales price and disposition date of any assets sold
- Business Insurance
    - Casualty loss insurance
    - Error and omissions
    - Other
- Interest Expense

-
    - Mortgage interest on building owned by business
    - Business loan interest
    - Investment expense and interest
- Professional fees
    - Lawyers, accountants, and consultants
- Office supplies
    - Pens, paper, staples, and other consumables
- Rent Expense
    - Office space rent
    - Business-use vehicle lease expense
    - Other
- Office-in-home
    - Square footage of office space
    - Total square footage of home
    - Hours of use, if operating an in-home daycare
    - Mortgage interest or rent paid
    - Homeowner's or renters' insurance
    - Utilities
    - Cost of home, separate improvements and first date of business use
- Wages paid to employees
    - Form W-2 and W-3
    - Federal and state payroll returns (Form 940, Form 941, etc.)

        Employee benefit expense (This is to be aligned with "Wages paid to employees")

        Contractors

        Form 1099-MISC

        Form 1096
- Other Expenses
    - Repairs, maintenance of office facility, etc.

- o Estimated tax payments made
- o Other business-related expenses

> Health insurance (Needs to be aligned with "Other expenses")
>
> Premiums paid to cover the sole-proprietor and family
>
> Premiums paid on behalf of partners and S corporation shareholders
>
> Information on spouse's employer provided insurance

I know this is a long list. It will ensure you and your bookkeeper are prepared. If you take the time each month to keep these documents organized and safe, when it comes time for taxes you will not need to look through everything to find what you need.

I encourage you to keep your business organized and in good shape. Make sure you keep your personal finances separate from your business finances. This includes separate bank accounts.

Before it is time to prepare for tax time, you should review the accounts receivable and inventory balances. This should be done at least quarterly. However, you should do it every time before closing the books and preparing them for the next fiscal year. Also make sure you review all equipment purchases for the year.

Many times there are added or potential tax credits you may be eligible for. Here is a list of just a few, but you would want to check and see what credits you could get each year as they could change.

- Research and Development Credit
- Energy Tax Credit
- Disabled Access Credit
- Work Opportunity Tax Credit
- Healthcare Tax Credit

Of course, as you close the books you will make your adjusting entries and prepare your business for the upcoming year.

For more information with filing taxes for your small business you can check out the IRS website at: https://www.irs.gov/businesses/small-businesses-self-employed

Other Tax Deductions

As you may or may not know, when it comes to tax deductions for running your small business there are so many to think about. I compiled a list of some other types of deductions for you to consider.

- Employees' Pay – This can be deducted as long is the pay is in the form of cash, property, or services.

- Inventory (cost of Goods Sold) – If your business manufacture products or purchases products for resale you can deduct the cost of goods sold.

- Employee Benefits – Such benefits like healthcare, adoption assistance, education assistance, and life insurance can be deducted.

- Home Office – Make sure you have a dedicated room for your home office. You will need to calculate the square footage so that you can apply a percentage of your rent, mortgage, insurance, utilities, housekeeping, etc. That percentage can be deducted if you work out of your home.

- Auto Maintenance and Mileage – There are two ways to calculate this rate. You can use the standard mileage rate or the actual expenses paid. Be sure to use whichever gives you the greatest deduction.

- Advertising and Marketing – You can deduct the cost for marketing and advertising your business. This includes promotion costs for good publicity.

- Office Supplies – This can be anything you use for your office. Make sure you keep your receipt of all items. These are small day-to-day items.

- Education – This includes educating people about your business through seminars and trade shows. Also, if you have magazines, books, CD's and DVD's that relate to your business, they are 100% deductible.

- Professional Fees – This includes accountant, lawyer and consulting fees. They are 100% deductible.

- Travel Expenses – When the travel is business related it is mostly all 100% deductible. This includes airfare, hotels, and other road expenses. However, eating out can be deducted but only at 50%.

- Entertainment – This one can be tricky. If you are just going out with co-workers it is not deductible. However, if you bring a client or prospective client you can deduct 50%. Same goes for if you take them out for drinks as long as it is in a business setting or business meeting.

- Furniture – This is supposed to have a long lifespan. Therefore, you can either deduct the full cost of the furniture at one time or you can deduct the depreciation over several years.

- Office Equipment – This will be those big items such a fax machine, copier, or computer. They are also 100% deductible and can be deducted the same way as the furniture.

- Employee or Client Gifts – It is always nice to reward your employees or clients with a gift. These are 100% deductible up to $25 per year for each person.

- Startup Expenses (Capital Expenses) – You can deduct up to $5,000. This includes research costs that you incurred for creating your business.

- Taxes – That's right. Taxes that incurred through running your business can be deductible.

- Insurance Premiums – The credit, liability, malpractice, and workers' compensation premiums call all be deducted.

- Interest – The interest that you incur from mortgage, finance charges such as credit cards, payment plans, and interest on loans are 100% deductible.

- Software – This includes boxed, downloadable, and subscriptions. They are all deductible.

- Charitable Contributions – If the contribution is more than $250 you will need a letter from the organization verifying the contribution. If the donation is not money, you can visit the IRS website and look up Publication 561 - Determining the Value of Donated Property.

- Rent – If you rent and the property is used for your business you can deduct the rent. However, if you receive any of that rent as equity you are not able to deduct it.

- Freelancers – When you hire an independent contractor you can deduct their pay as a business expense.

- Repairs and Maintenance – When you run a business there will always be some repairs and maintenance that needs to be done for your business to still run smoothly. These are deductible.

- Licenses – License fees and regulatory fees are deductible.

- Etc. – There is so many more. With a little research, you could find deductions that you never knew existed.

Preparing W-2's for your employees

Many times when we start a business and have employees we do not know how to prepare the W-2's. That is why I want to set you up for success in this area. When an employee first starts working with your business, you need to have them file a W4 for employee or a W9 for independent contractor. This is the basis for starting the W-2 preparations.

Let's first start by checking all the information on the W-4. This form needs to be on file with your business at all times. If there are any changes that need to be made, such as an employee moved, then you will need them to file an updated form. To ensure that all the information is correct before preparing the W-2 it is a good idea to have all employees look over their W-4 to ensure it is up-to-date. This form changes each year. Therefore, in January you must provide this form to all your employees for the current year.

Gathering Information

Let's look at some of the basic information you will need from your business for each employee.

- Business Employee ID Number
- Name, Address, and Zip Code of the business
- Business State Tax ID Number

This information will be on every W-2 prepared by the business. It is a good idea to have it saved where you can find it easily whenever it is needed.

Now we need to gather information about each employee.

- Employee name, address, and social security number or other tax ID number
- Amount paid to the employee. (i.e. total wages, tips, and other compensation)
- Amount of federal income tax withheld
- Social security wages (only up to the maximum amount for the year)
- Medicare wages and tips and Medicare tax withheld
- Allocated tips paid
- Dependent care benefits paid and benefits taxable to the employee
- State wages, tips, and income taxes withheld for each state the employee worked
- Local wages and tips paid and local income tax withheld

Review and Creating your W-2's

Keep in mind, every employee who worked for you during the year must get a W-2 from the business. This includes if they only worked for you one day. They will still receive a W-2.

There are many ways you can get the W-2 forms needed for printing. You can buy them from your local office supply store, your CPA, a tax or accounting software, and from the IRS. However, W2's are not downloadable from the IRS website.

There are a few options for printing your W-2 forms.

- Accounting Software – you may need to purchase an add-on for this processing feature
- Tax preparation Software – check to see if it is included with the software you are using.
- Purchase W2 forms

If you are able to, it is easier to use accounting software with the payroll feature. Simply get the add-on and all the work is done for you. Your accounting software will keep track of all the information for you and at the end of the year you will need to review to make sure it is accurate before printing.

Regardless of which method you use, you should also have a W-3 transmission form. A W-3 must be submitted to the IRS, which will show the totals of the W-2's.

Distribution of the W-2's

Many businesses have different ways of distributing the W-2's. Remember, all W-2's must be out no later than January 31st.

There are two ways that W-2's can be distributed. You can choose to either mail them or have the employee pick them up. However, many businesses are making the W-2 more accessible on a secured business website. This allows employees to print out their own W-2 for filing taxes. It also helps to ensure employees will not lose their W-2 and need a copy from the employer.

Filing W-2 and W-3 Forms

Now that you have gotten all of your W-2's out to the employees, it is time to decide how you are going to file them with the Social Security Administration. You will need to file form W-3 complete with copy A of each W-2 for your employees.

There are two ways to file these forms.

1. File online at the business services online section of the Social Security website. You will need to register first to file electronically.
2. Mail completed forms W-2 and W-3 to the Social Security Administration.

Also, if the employee pays state taxes, then copy 1 of the W-2 will get sent to the state taxing authority for every state they worked in and paid taxes to.

Chapter 10 – Small Business Checklist

So many times we ask ourselves, "What do we need to do? When do we need to do it?" That is what this chapter will help us answer. Here is a checklist that will help your bookkeeper know when to perform each task to help you run your business smoothly.

Daily Bookkeeping Tasks:

- Check Cash Position
    - Cash is like the fuel to your company. Therefore, you never want to run out of cash to operate your business with.

Weekly Bookkeeping Tasks

- Record Transactions
- Document and File Receipts
- Review Unpaid Bills From your Vendors
- Pay Vendors and Sign Checks
- Prepare and Send Invoices
- Review Projected Cash Flow

Monthly Bookkeeping Tasks

- Balance the Business Checkbook
- Review Past-Due ("Aged") Receivables
- Analyze Inventory Status
- Process or Review Payroll and Approve Tax Payments

- Review Actual Profit and Loss vs. Budget vs. Prior Years
- Review Month-End Balance Sheet vs. Prior Period

Quarterly Bookkeeping Tasks

- Prepare/Review Revised Annual P&L Estimate
- Review Quarterly Payroll Reports and Make Payments
- Review Sales Tax and Make Quarterly Payments
- Compute Estimated Income Tax and Make Payment

Annual Bookkeeping Tasks

- Review Past-Due Receivables
- Review Inventory
- Fill Out IRS Forms W-2 and 1099-MISC
- Review and Approve Full-Year Financial Reports and Tax Returns

This checklist is only an example. With it, you can get started and on your way to becoming organized. As your business progresses and you meet with your bookkeeper, you may want to add to or take away from this checklist. It is here to act as a guide.

As you perform these tasks weekly, monthly, quarterly, or annually you may want to change it and perform some tasks more frequently. Sometimes when you are first starting out it is a good idea to run reports on a monthly basis. This will give you a better understanding of how you are doing each month.

Chapter 11 – Bookkeeping tips for your Small Business

I want to take a few minutes to go over a few tips that you can follow. These tips will not only make things easier for you, as the business owner, but your bookkeeper will have an easier time as well.

Bookkeeping does not need to feel like a nightmare. With a little planning, you can have your records accurate and complete at all times.

Tip 1: Keep Accurate Records

Most of your day-to-day business activities are handled and tracked through your online banking. However, the most important aspect is that your financial records are all kept in one place. This way you do not need to scramble to meet requests.

Granted, online banking will make it simple to track debits and credits. This does not mean you do not need some sort of bookkeeping records. It is important to know how the money was spent. Therefore, the records need to track the inflow and outflow of cash. This includes purchases with a credit card, when reimbursements are made to employees, etc.

Making a good investment in a cash basis accounting software will help with this tracking system.

Tip 2: Sort and File Receipts

In your business, you will have a lot of receipts on a daily or monthly basis. Do not throw these away. However, filing them can be stressful. Keep in mind, if you file them and keep them organized it will eliminate the headaches in the future. It is vital that you keep all receipts for your business, although receipt accounts go well beyond just keeping the receipts.

Keep your receipts organized. Over time the ink on the receipts will fade. That's why it can be good to photocopy or scan your receipts. Then organize them by date to correspond with your detailed financial records. Many bookkeeping software will allow for you to scan and attach the receipt to the transactions made. This is a great feature that will help you keep track of all the receipts. However, even if the receipt is attached, you should still keep the scanned copy in case something happens with the software or it does not upload properly.

When keeping all your receipts, it will help reduce the headaches of tax time. If any of your items are tax deductible, you will need these receipts. Therefore, you should highlight the date and make notes about the reason for the expense. If you photocopy the receipt you will have room to make all the notes on the page with the receipt.

Tip 3: Collect Applicable Taxes

I cannot stress this enough. Taxes need to be taken out at the time of the sale or when payroll is generated. Just like with the receipts, the longer you go between the transactions, the more chances for errors. Be sure to take care of the taxes when they occur.

You need to collect or apply taxes as soon as they occur, such as when a sale is made or payroll is generated. This will ensure:

1. Your business is not liable for a lump sum of taxes at the end of the year, and
2. Your business will not incur penalties due to delayed tax payments.

That's right. If the taxes are delayed after they incur, then the IRS will charge you a late penalty.

Tip 4: Do Accurate Invoicing

Even though invoices are to let your clients know when to make payments, there is much more to it than that. An invoice is a record of terms of a transaction. Because of this, it is important that the information is accurate and complete. There is a difference between an invoice and a receipt. An invoice is what you will give to your clients letting them know how much and when to make payments to your business. You can also consider these as future inflows of cash. Receipts are your business expenses, or the outflows of cash.

Tip 5: Get Donation and Contribution Receipts

There are tax benefits in donating to outside organizations, although to take advantage of these tax benefits you will need to get a receipt for verification of the donation. Each receipt should have how much the donation is worth.

There are some donations that require more than a check to ensure their validity. If the donation is over a specific amount, then a receipt is required.

Requesting a receipt seems like a simple request. Remember, that receipt could mean the difference between a tax write-off or the write-off being denied.

When in doubt, get a receipt. In this way you will always be covered for your contribution.

Tip 6: Schedule Profit and Loss Statements

A great way to check the health of your company is a Profit and Loss Statement. This statement will provide an overview of many areas of the business. It can help summarize the business activity for a given period. That means you can have a P&L scheduled monthly, quarterly, or annually. It depends on the direction of your business.

Your bookkeeper or accountant may find discrepancies in the P&L as each one is pulled. It is important to have these printed to give them an idea which period of time that discrepancy occurred so that it can be corrected.

The P&L can also be key to finding and deciphering other records that you keep for your business.

These six helpful tips are a great way to make it easier for your business and bookkeeper. Some of the simplest tasks can be the most important. It will make it easier to perform each of these tasks if you follow a standard schedule of tasks to remind you of what needs to be done and when.

Proper and responsible time management of any task is the key ingredient for success. This is especially true in bookkeeping and accounting. Most of that scary feeling and large bit of time comes from poor preparation. Keep your business records accurate and organized on a daily basis. This will eliminate so much frustration along the way.

Conclusion

This book has given you the tools to better understand not only your bookkeeper, but your business as well. These are all areas that you, as a business owner, need to know and understand.

Each area that we have covered has a purpose. When you work hand-in-hand with your bookkeeper, you will see the light at the end of the tunnel.

I mentioned in the beginning, "It is not the business owner that runs the business. It is the business owner teamed up with the bookkeeper that truly runs the business."

I want to take a minute to breakdown that statement. As the business owner, you have the power to make the decisions that will move your business forward. Your business will succeed or fail based on your decisions.

Your bookkeeper is the gate keeper. They hold the power over the financial health of your business. With their mighty power, you can have all the financial statements you need when you need them. They can also ensure that all the transactions are correct.

As a team, you are unstoppable. Your bookkeeper can ensure you have what is needed to move your business in the right direction. They can also help guide you in making the right decisions. With the proper analysis and ratios, you can predict the future if the trend is steady.

Now I have empowered you to be on the same level as your bookkeeper and accountant.

If you have not started your business yet, but you are thinking about it and currently doing the research for your business, then this is a great place to start.

With the knowledge that you have learned, you will also be better prepared to add your financials to your business plan and pitch deck.

Best of luck to all your endeavors. I look forward to seeing your business up and running and hearing about the great success you will be having.

Part 2: Accounting

The Ultimate Guide to Accounting for Beginners – Learn the Basic Accounting Principles

Introduction

This book is intended for people who want to know something about the fundamentals of financial accounting without becoming an accountant. Many people are in this position; small business owners, employers, employees, business owners, stockholders, investors, and many, many more. Most of these folks do not need a deep understanding of accounting, they just need to learn what accounting is and how they should be using it. Just as important, they need to understand what accountants are talking about in their reports. They must learn the vocabulary and the most important terms. The product of accounting is information, important information for that wide range of stakeholders.

We will examine this subject in some detail, discussing accounting fundamentals, the various areas where accounting professionals work and the information they produce. We will also examine the measures and ratios that accountants use to analyze an organization's performance and the important relationship between time and money. The fact that information is the product of accounting will remain foremost in this book.

Chapter 1 - Accounting is Different From Bookkeeping

Accounting is not bookkeeping. Bookkeeping concentrates on recording the organization's financial activities, whatever the business in which they are engaged. Maybe that is retail sales, home construction or manufacturing. No matter what business activity is taking place, someone must keep track of the transactions; selling, buying, repairing equipment, everything of significance. And in fact, even individuals must learn about accounting and must do certain bookkeeping tasks for their own personal finances, like balancing their checkbook and establishing personal budgets.

If the business is engaged in retail sales, bookkeepers record every sale, every purchase of inventory and every employee's pay. That is bookkeeping.

Accountants take this information and analyze, summarize and report the results. Remember, the product of accounting is information. This information is vital to management for their operating and investment decisions. Management must know how much money the business has, how much inventory it holds, how many employees are retained and how much they are being paid.

The viewpoint of a bookkeeper is the details. The viewpoint of an accountant is much broader and at a higher level. The accountant must be able to advise management on many decisions; how many more employees can be hired, what taxes are due and how to minimize them, analyzing investment decisions, and so forth.

Let's look at an example. Riverside Machine Company is a small manufacturer of components for the automobile industry. Their clients include almost all of the automobile manufacturers, and they are very busy when the industry is thriving.

The owners of Riverside are concerned about reducing manufacturing costs for a certain type of part that requires a lot of machining on several different types of machines. The engineers have determined that they can increase the rate of production by installing robots to load and unload the machines and transfer parts between them. The company has several robotic systems in operation now and is confident of their ability to incorporate these new robots. Currently, there is a serious backlog of work for these machines and improving the workflow would allow faster delivery with less overtime and not needing to work weekends to maintain production.

The engineers have determined all the necessary information related to this investment in terms of robot costs, tools needed by the robots, increases in production rate and effect on delivery time. They then sit down with the accounting experts to compute the improvements in cost, reductions in labor costs, shortening of delivery time and so forth. The accountant then uses all of this information to compute the effects on the firm's financial performance and profitability.

In most companies, the accountants compute a value for "Internal Rate of Return" for decisions by management. This rate of return serves as a threshold for new projects. It becomes one of the considerations used by management to decide whether or not to make the investment, in this case, in the new robots. Other considerations of course include delivery improvements, customer satisfaction, product quality and several others. That is a proper role for the accountant working with the engineers.

In addition to being a source of reliable financial information on these kinds of decisions, the accounting department also acts as what can be described as a "Scorekeeper", by monitoring costs and revenues, leading to profitability for the firm. This information is reported to management on a regular basis to help guide ongoing management decisions. The accountants cannot do much at all to influence the profitability of the firm directly, but their role is to report findings to management for them to make decisions.

The accounting function also leads the efforts at budgeting and budget reporting. These are more examples of the accounting product of information. These reports are available in varying levels of detail for publically owned companies and non-profit organizations. Privately owned companies are not required to publish these reports, except for those required by the government, regulatory and taxing authorities.

In their role as providers of information, they are often called upon for informed recommendations to help management decision making.

Chapter 2 - Understanding the Vocabulary

Every special area of interest has its own vocabulary, and accounting is the same. Many of the words used will be familiar to the reader but may have certain shades of meaning that are important. We need to understand this vocabulary. Here are some key definitions that are important to the accounting function.

Asset: an asset is anything the organization owns that helps it accomplish its mission. For a fast food restaurant, the grill or stove in the kitchen area is an asset. For a retail store, the inventory in the back room is an asset, along with display cases and shelves.

Liability: a liability is anything the organization owes to someone else. Unpaid wages to employees is a liability, taxes owed to the local government is a liability, unpaid insurance premiums for employee healthcare policies is a liability, bills for inventory that have not been paid is a liability.

Equity: equity is a measure of the claim of someone on the assets of the organization, such as liabilities (claims by the person or entity to whom the liability is owed, such as loans from a bank) and the investment by the owners of the organization.

Income: money flowing into the organization from its operations in whatever the line of business might be, for example, sales in a fast food restaurant, or rent collected on property the business owns.

Expense: this is the amount of money the organization needs to spend in order to carry out its operations. This represents payments to asset and service providers. For example, payments to a supplier of inventory items for a retail store.

Distributions: outflows of money to owners or stockholders, or bonuses to employees at the end of the year, for example.

Cash Flow: the term cash flow represents the money flowing through the operation, essentially income minus expenses. You can imagine a stream of money flowing into the organization with small streams going out as distributaries to pay for liabilities. The flow that is moving through this stream is the cash flow. How much is left at the end of the process is the profit for the firm.

Overhead: this is a group of costs not directly associated with the major function of the organization but necessary in order to make the organization accomplish its goals. For example, in a hospital, the janitorial staff that cleans and sanitizes the buildings, rooms and equipment are not directly associated with the hospital's patients, but they are absolutely essential. The labor and other costs like cleaning and sanitizing supplies are part of the organization's overhead. All the other myriad of costs like electricity, lighting, lawn maintenance, and even sweeping the parking lot are essential but not directly tied to the patients and their care. The accounting office is considered overhead for any organization not involved in the Public Accounting business.

GAAP: This is the term used to describe the Generally Accepted Accounting Principles. This is a set of 'rules' for the accounting profession, which must be followed to assure an accurate description of the financial activities of the organization. GAAP applies to all organizations that function in commerce, public service, and all other sectors of the general economy. Following these GAAP rules assures the public, the stockholders, the donors to non-profit organizations, the owners, employees and the taxing and regulatory authorities that the accounting for the organization is done in accordance with the proper methods and systems.

Each country establishes its own accounting standards but there exists an International Accounting Standards Board responsible for establishing and accrediting accounting standards for all nations who subscribe. Similarly, many countries establish similar Boards, to promulgate and enforce standards through certification and audit systems. These are in the form of standards, conventions and rules. Companies are not necessarily required to follow them but any publicly traded company must conform to the established Accounting Practices.

Chapter 3 – Accounting Reports: The Income Statement

Remember that the product of accounting is information. The three most common forms for that information are the "Income Statement", the "Balance Sheet", and the "Cash Flow Statement." Every organization uses some form of these three documents and usually all three. We will explore the Balance Sheet in Chapter 4 and the Cash Flow Statement in Chapter 5.

The Income Statement or Profit and Loss Statement (or P&L statement) can be imagined as a video tape of the organization over some period of time, like a month, six months or a year. This statement tells management how the firm is doing from the standpoint of "Are we making money or not?" Of course, this is a very fundamental question, since after a number of periods of losses, the firm will no longer be viable and will go out of business.

The most important use of the Income Statement is to compare it with prior periods and with the period budget. If management has determined that the firm must meet certain performance levels, they need the answer to the question above; "How are we doing compared with our goals and budget?" Each organization has an established and agreed upon budget. The budget contains allocations of resources for all of the activities of the organization, from sales, purchases of materials for sale or production, employee salaries and benefits and even overhead items like electricity and water.

These budgets are set up, usually each year, to guide the managers and supervisors in what decisions can be made to commit resources like money and labour, and for what purposes. Based on this budget, which has been agreed upon by management, it acts as a steering mechanism for the firm's operations. The periodic P&L reports represent the Accounting function's role in keeping score. Here is an example of a P&L Statement or an Income Statement. We will look at each of these entries to see what they represent, based on The Martin Company.

THE MARTIN COMPANY, INC.
INCOME STATEMENT
(FIRST HALF, 2014)
JANUARY 1, 2014 THROUGH JUNE 30, 2014
(all amounts in thousands of dollars)

Sales, Gross: $116,410

Less: Returns and Allowances: $3,075

Net Sales: $113,335

Less Cost of Goods Sold: $78,683

Less Current Depreciation Charges: $1,450

Gross Profit: $33,202

Operating Expenses

Selling and Promotion: $18,005

General and Administration: $8,910

Total Operating Expenses: $26,915

Operating Profit: $6,287

(Gross Profit minus Operating Expense)

Other Income and Expense

Interest and Dividend Income: $363

less: Interest Expense: $917

Net Interest Expense: $554

Profit Before Taxes: $5,733

Taxes on Income at 35%: $2,007

Net Profit: $3,726

This P&L or Income Statement is for the Martin Company. The Martin Company manufacturers small household appliances, which are sold through distributors under Martin's label and major discount and department stores under their labels. Manufacturing operations are located in a small town in the Midwest. The key technologies employed by the firm include manufacturing of fractional horsepower motors, injection molding of plastic parts and machining of miscellaneous small metal parts such as shafts, armatures and gears as well as assembly of the products, packaging and shipping them to customers.

As it says at the top, this report covers the first half of the year. For this company, their budget year is a calendar year. Some organizations may use other budget years. Government organizations often use October 1 through September 30 as a budget year. A mid-year report is very valuable to management, to keep track of performance, especially in complex organizations.

Total Sales; The first line entered is the total sales for that period. This is the value of products shipped to customers. In some cases, there may be returns from customers for any number of reasons; wrong color, wrong address, quality issues, and so forth. This is recorded as Returns and Allowances and is subtracted from Gross Sales resulting in Net Sales.

Cost of Goods Sold; The line labeled Cost of Goods Sold represents the cost that Martin incurred in producing the products shipped during that period. That will include the materials and components purchased, the labor used to produce these products and may include machine time if that is the procedure for Martin Company.

Depreciation; Martin Company must also account for the wear and tear on their productive assets ranging from big, expensive plastic injection molding machines to company vehicles. This is a real cost that must be accounted for but is not a cash expense. It is determined by the accounting office and along with the Cost of Goods Sold, reduces the net sales to give the amount of Gross Profit. This loss of value of assets is called depreciation and is subtracted from sales, even though it is not a cash expense. Depreciation will be covered in a later section.

Operating Expenses; However, this is not the complete picture of costs incurred. The items labeled Operating Expenses include the salaries of the supervisors, managers, sales representatives, shipping operators, energy costs like electric power and gas, office expenses for papers, copiers, and the myriad of other costs necessary to produce the products that generate sales income. In some companies, this lump of costs may be referred to as "Overhead." Overhead is a necessary expense and must be included in the budget and in P&L statement. Managers and supervisors work hard to keep Overhead costs to a minimum. Overhead also includes taxes paid on the real estate and other ad valorum taxes. These amounts are shown as Selling and Promotion as well as General and Administrative or G&A. G&A usually includes the Overhead costs.

Operating Profit; After accounting for the Operating Expenses, we are left with the Operating Profit. Operating Profit is the first measure of how effective Martin Company is in carrying out its main objective, making and selling products. Operating Profit is the Gross Profit minus the Operating Expenses.

Other Income and Expense; But, Martin Company must also take into account the other costs such as interest on loans they need to purchase equipment and materials. They may have other incidental income from sources like investments, rental property receipts and royalties. These are all included in the P&L statement but are not part of the major business, making and selling products.

Profit Before Taxes; When all of that is included, we see the Profit Before Taxes or PBT. That profit must be reduced by the taxes paid on the sales and other income, and we finally get to see the profits resulting from the major business of Martin. This is what managers call the "Bottom Line."

Managers and supervisors are vitally concerned with how the P&L Statement compares with the budget and how it is changing over time. Are we earning more profit this year than we did in the same period last year and in prior years? Continual growth in profit makes it possible of Martin to stay in business, producing products, serving customers and employing people. It is also essential to being able to expand the business, adding more products and investing in advanced technologies that customers demand.

Chapter 4 - The Balance Sheet

A short description of the Balance Sheet is that it states "What we own and what we owe." Think of the Balance Sheet as a photograph of the business at a point in time. Just as the Income Statement is a recording of progress over time, the Balance Sheet gives us a picture of the company at some requested time, say at the end of the year or mid-year as shown here for the Martin Company. The Balance Sheet may also be called the Position Statement.

THE MARTIN COMPANY, INC.

BALANCE SHEET

AS OF JUNE 30, 2014

Assets in $,000's,

Current Assets

Cash: $2,493

Accounts Receivable: $18,610

Inventory: $9,308

Prepaids: $780

Total Current Assets:$31,191

Long Term Assets

Investments: $7,300

Property and Equipment: $22,730

Less Accumulated Depreciation ($7,382)

Intangibles: $2,670

Total Long Term Assets: $29,044

Total Assets: $60,235

LIABILITIES AND OWNER'S EQUITY, in $,000's

Current Liabilities

Accounts Payable: $5,350

Salaries and Benefits Payable: $2,480

Taxes Payable: $1,855

Notes Payable within 1 year: $5,000

Total Current Liabilities: $14,685

Long Term Debt: $15,000

Owner's Equity

Invested Capital: $15,000

Retained Earnings: $15,550

Total Owner's Equity: $30,550

Total Liabilities and Owner's Equity: $60,235

We will describe each of these line items in the order shown on the Balance Sheet. Just as with the Income Statement, all these figures are shown in thousands.

Assets are "What we Own"

Current Items

Current Assets; those assets which we can access quickly, such as 90 days.

Cash; represents money in demand deposits, like a checking account, needed for paying current bills like utilities and wages. A company's cash may also be held in short term investments like Certificates of Deposit with maturity dates of one year or less.

Accounts Receivable; the money we have billed to customers but have not yet received. If we receive a check in the mail today paying an invoice for products shipped, the amount in the Accounts Receivable will be decreased by that amount and the Cash Account will be increased by the same amount.

Inventory; represents all the finished goods that have been produced and are awaiting shipment, along with all of the material that is currently being worked on and all of the raw materials on hand. Other items like processing materials and maintenance supplies, office supplies and so forth are included here.

Prepaids; is another interesting account. When Martin Company paid the property taxes for this year, say in January that is called a prepaid, since that expense will last for the entire year. Insurance premiums, investments in retirement plans and so forth are usually included as prepaids.

The amount of current assets for Martin Company, $31,191, is the total for current assets.

Long Term Items

Long Term Assets are the fixed assets that will last for many accounting periods. For instance, if Martin has purchased an interest in another company, that represents an investment. Similarly, stocks, bonds and other financial instruments are categorized as investments. These are non-depreciable assets. We will cover depreciation next, under Property and Equipment

Property and Equipment; the value of all the land, buildings, warehouses, machinery used in production and all the other equipment that has been purchased in the past and is or could be used in production, shipping and sales of Martin Company's products. However, all of this reflects past purchases, and except for land but including buildings, has a finite lifetime. A plastic injection-molding machine, bought new four years ago, will no longer be valuable at some time in the future. The loss in value can be due to wear and tear and even technological obsolescence. When it loses all its value, it will be taken out of production and perhaps sold for its scrap value. This decrease in value is recognized through the accounting process called depreciation.

Essentially all assets in the company are continuously losing value, either through wear out, age or technological advances. For instance, the computer system used to track production is, like all other computer and high technology assets, becoming obsolete continuously. Assets are being consumed by time, technology or wear. The building for example, has a finite lifetime. At some point, Martin Company will need to replace the building or at least make a major refurbishment, just because of its age. If no new long-term assets are purchased, the value of the total Property and Equipment line will decrease each period to reflect depreciation.

Depreciation: The costs for depreciation are actual costs in that they reflect the diminishment in value of an asset through its use or age. These depreciation costs are not actual cash costs, that is, they do not represent funds flowing out of the firm but they are necessary costs incurred in order to produce products or services. These depreciation charges are generally included in a separate line in the P&L Statement, as shown above.

The methods used for allocating the cost of an asset over its lifetime, that is depreciation are beyond the scope of this book. However, the methods used are frequently set by the taxing authority, since it reduces the profit before taxes and hence, the amount of tax paid. It also affects any ad valorem taxes on property and equipment.

Intangibles; is a general category for all the other assets of the firm such as royalties on patents held by the company, trademarks, copyrights, organization costs, and more. These Intangible Assets may have infinite lifetime, with respect to the existence of the company, and are usually not subject to depreciation.

The total of Current and Long term Assets gives the total asset value of the firm. For our example of Martin Company, this amounts to about 60 million dollars, ($60,235,000). This number will appear again in the other side of the Balance Sheet where the liabilities are shown. Remember that the Balance Sheet shows what we own and what we owe. The liabilities are what we owe. We can also think of Liabilities as the source of the capital we have invested to purchase land, buildings, equipment, inventory and the like, our assets.

Liabilities - "What we Owe"

What we owe is funds owed to someone outside the firm or to the owners of the firm. These are all called liabilities because sooner or later, they must be paid.

Current Liabilities Current Liabilities are those which must be paid within a year or less. Accounts payable are the bills we have received but not yet paid, for anything we have purchased. Raw materials, purchased parts, shipping invoices, office supplies, lease payments for things like a copy machine, all fall under the umbrella of Current Liabilities.

Salaries and Benefits Payable; are just that. We do not pay employees every day. We must show on the balance sheet the amounts that have been accrued and will be paid in the next payment cycle. Outstanding invoices for things like employee medical and life insurance, workers compensation insurance premiums and salaries for supervisors and executives are all included in Salaries and Benefits Payable. Clearly, these fit the description of what we owe.

Taxes; may be accrued and this line represents the acknowledgment of this debt. Taxes may be income taxes for the firm, employee withholding taxes for social security or employee income tax, local taxes including property and ad valorem taxes and so forth. This is a debt that must be paid.

Notes Payable within 1 year; represents any short term borrowing Martin Company may have done for whatever purpose and is due within the next twelve months. For example, a company may choose to borrow funds to finance an increase in inventory. These are short-term notes.

The sum of these is the total of Current Liabilities. Most companies borrow some amounts of money to pay for things like raw materials inventory in anticipation of a seasonal or cyclical increase in sales.

Long Term Debt is for things like bonds we may have sold to raise capital, bank or other financing company loans due beyond the next year. Long Term Debt and Current Liabilities is the amount the firm owes to entities outside of the firm.

Invested Capital; is the money the owners contributed in order to start the firm and if, at any point since, the owners have invested more money to expand or maintain the business. This may have taken place a number of years ago or may be invested periodically, as the owners choose to put more money into the business.

Retained Earnings; is not cash in the bank. It is the value of the firm built up during its years of existence. It represents the money not distributed to owners or spent to maintain operations, like buying raw material. It is the profits retained and used to buy assets like property and equipment, invest in long term assets such as production equipment, buildings and parking lots.

The total of Invested Capital and Retained Earnings represents the owners' share of the business. For Martin Company, the total is $60,235,000. Notice that this is exactly equal to the total assets shown above. The fact that these two numbers are equal is not an accident. This equality is why this report is called the Balance Sheet. It shows the balance between what we own and what we owe. Chapter 6 will discuss that balance further, as the Accounting Equation.

Chapter 5 – The Cash Flow Statement

Every organization depends on its immediate cash reserves to pay its bills. This is not different from a personal household, where the householder must keep money in a savings or checking account to pay all the bills that are due. On some occasions, the individual may choose to keep cash but that is not recommended because of the risk of loss or theft. Companies and organizations do not pay in cash for the same reasons.

What is important to any organization or individual is that there is sufficient money flowing into the cash account to cover current liabilities. The flow of money into and out of the organization is called its Cash Flow, and is reported on the Cash Flow Statement.

For private and public owned firms, for-profit companies, the primary source of revenue is the firm's operations. Whether it is in the manufacturing, retailing, servicing or any other sector, its operations are the reason the firm exists. For non-profits and charitable organizations, the main income is from donations and fund raising. That is their operations equivalent.

There are usually three streams of cash flow reported, if the organization is involved in all three. They are:

1) Cash flow from operations

2) Cash flow from investments

3) Cash flow from financing activities

Cash Flow from Operations

Operations cash flow is just that; cash flowing into and out of the operations of the organization. The cash flow statements are taken directly from the Income Statement and the Balance Sheet. We will use Martin Company as our example. Many organizations have different rules for determining cash flow.

For Martin, remember their Income Statement showed cash at $2,493,000 shown in thousands as $2,493. There are several other lines for which we must account. Accountants base the cash flow statement Operating Profit, PBT or Profit Before taxes. The cash shown is part of that PBT, at $5,733.

Martin has incurred depreciation charges but these are not cash expenditures so they must be added back into the cash flow. Receivables are also liquid assets and represent cash flow in the near future.

Inventories represent cash already spent or committed so they do not add to cash flow, at least not until they are used in operations and sold as products. However, some firms may include inventory in cash flow. That is determined by the organization.

Similarly, accounts payable and any other accrued liabilities must also be subtracted from net income since they are liabilities that must be paid with cash. These might be salaries and wages due at the end of the period.

The final amount represents the Net Cash Flow from Operations for Martin Company for that period. The accountants then compare that with the same cash flow from the previous period to see if cash is increasing or decreasing. Organizations always want the cash flow to increase, since that represents their ability to meet their obligations, pay the owners and lenders and certainly, to grow the business by expansion.

Cash Flow from Investing

However, this is not the only user of cash. The company must pay for any assets it purchases during the period or funds used to pay for assets previously purchased. This is the Cash Flow From Investing, in this case, investing in plant and equipment. Any capital assets acquired during this period must be shown in this line item.

In the case of The Martin Company, no new assets were acquired during this period so that entry is zero.

Cash Flow from Financing Activities

The company must also meet its long-term liabilities which may be in the form of long-term notes it has issued in the past and must be repaid. For a publicly owned organization, any dividends also consume cash and they appear under financing activities, since selling stock is a means to finance the company. In the same way, for privately held organizations, any payments to the owners are made from cash so they must be included in the cash flow statement.

Cash Flow Statement The Martin Company

January 1, 2014 through June 30, 2014

(All amounts in thousands of dollars)

Cash Flow from Operations	($000's dollars
Operating Profit	6,287
Depreciation	1,450
Accounts Receivable	18,610
Inventory	(9,308)
Accounts Payable	(5,350)
Salaries and Benefits Payable	(2,480)
Taxes Payable	(1,855)
Net Cash Flow from Operations	**7,354**
Cash Flow from Investing	
None for this period	
Cash Flow from Financing Activities	
Interest and Dividend Income	363
Interest Expense	(917)
Net Interest Expense	(554)
Net Cash from Financing Activities	**(554)**
Total Cash Flow at End of Period	**6,800**

Chapter 6 – The Accounting Equation

The Accounting Equation is probably the most fundamental part of accounting as it is done in modern times. It captures the concept described in the Balance Sheet. That concept is that for any going concern, what the concern owns comes from only two sources, funds borrowed, expressed as liabilities and funds owed to the owners, their equity.

Assets = Liabilities + Owner's Equity

This equation is often expressed in its expanded form;

Assets = Liabilities+ Owner's Capital+ Revenues- Expenses- Owner Draws

In this form, it describes more of the operations of the firm. The assets of the firm come from:

Liabilities; money contributed by entities outside the firm such as long term and short term loans from banks or investment companies, sale of stock, bonds sold, and so forth.

Owner's Capital; the funds supplied by the owners and the profits generated by the operations.

Shareholder Stock; owners can be shareholders of common or preferred stocks, frequently sold on a stock exchange

Revenues; money generated by the operations of the firm and other sources of revenue or income

Expenses; costs incurred in the operation of the firm such as material, labor and all the other expenses

Owner Draws; money withdrawn from the company and paid to the owners, as profits withdrawn, dividends, bonuses or in any other form.

One can see that the expanded version better describes the operation of the firm in carrying out its business, whether that business is retail sales, manufacturing, mining, or any other activity designed to generate revenues and profits. Even hospitals and other service businesses follow this same expanded model.

Revenues are generated, expenses incurred and paid, and profits distributed. Of course, this appears very much different for all of the various business models under which firms operate. This expanded equation describes the business models for large, international firms that are publicly owned by stockholders, all the way down to the small privately owned construction firms, farms or service business owned and operated by self-employed entrepreneurs. Every organization can be seen to operate exactly by this accounting equation.

For example, Riverside Machine Company, illustrated in Chapter 1, The Martin Company illustrated in Chapters 3, 4 and 5 and all the other firms in whatever businesses one can imagine, all follow this universal accounting equation. It truly is universal in its application, for companies and organizations of all sizes, in all industries, in all countries in the world. This is truly the fundamental equation of accounting.

And, all accounting and accountants, in all these businesses must follow the earlier discussed GAAP, generally accepted accounting principles establish by authorities and certification bodies.

Banks, investment firms, investment fund managers, and everyone else in all market sectors are subject to this universal fundamental equation. We will see this in the subsequent chapters as we describe the various accounting professionals, their functions and responsibilities in all aspects of the accounting world.

Chapter 7 – The CPA and Public Accounting

Probably the most recognized accounting professionals are the CPAs, the Certified Public Accountants. These professionals may work for very large accounting firms like PriceWaterhouseCoopers® or KPMG®, two internationally known and respected accounting firms with offices in most countries around the world or the small one or two person offices in almost every city and town in every nation. CPAs perform many valuable services for all types of businesses and organizations. A church, for example, must file and pay the required payroll taxes for all employees on a timely basis. CPAs can set up the accounting systems for a church secretary or bookkeeper to use in meeting these requirements.

Similarly, any organization must establish responsibility and authority for internal auditing. Auditing in general means that the organization must carry out the accounting function in accordance with established standards and must assure management that the records are being kept accurately and in compliance with these standards and laws. This internal auditing function is normally carried out by employees of the organization who are educated, trained and hired for that purpose, usually within the organization's financial control office. This internal auditing task may also be outsourced to an independent firm such as a CPA company.

External auditing is required by law for all publicly owned companies and other organizations. External auditing must be carried out by a qualified external authority, who is not part of the organization being audited. CPA's can serve as these Independent External Auditors. They must represent an independent third party, a role most often carried out by an organization in business as CPAs or External Auditors. These can be small, individual business firms or large multinational companies, like those mentioned above and many more.

For publicly owned companies, that is firms who sell stock certificates, privately or through a stock market, the external audit report is extremely important and is addressed to the stockholders. For privately held firms, the report is addressed to the owners and the highest level of management. Shareholders rely on the external audit report to assure them that the firm is carrying out its accounting for the business activities in accordance with the GAAP or other applicable standards.

For non-profits and charitable organizations, the report is addressed to the Board of Directors.

Sharon Haas for example, is a graduate of a mid-western university with a degree in Business Administration where she majored in accounting and an MBA with a focus on Accounting and Finance. She has ten years experience in accounting for a medium sized manufacturing firm in Chicago, Illinois. The State of Illinois as most other states in the US requires 150 hours of education to qualify for the CPA certificate and license. The MBA is frequently used to meet this requirement. Many states also have a requirement for continuing education to maintain the CPA license. Sharon passed the required examination and was issued her license after her graduate studies.

At present, she works as an external auditor for one of the multinational CPA firms, in their office in Cleveland, Ohio. Her client assignments are a number of firms in Ohio, Michigan, Wisconsin and Illinois. She is a member of AICPA, the American Institute of CPAs.

As an external auditor, she maintains a relationship with her client firms, providing consultant services in the areas of taxes, investments, capital purchases and accounting. Every year, she visits each client firm to carry out her external audit duties. She has an assistant who travels with her, helping in the audit duties and in preparing the annual audit report.

Sharon enjoys her work with both her employer and her clients. She says there is never a dull day; every day brings on new questions and different challenges.

One of the most important responsibilities that Sharon and all other external auditors have is to be careful with is to maintain the position of an objective outside authority. Sharon, like most professionals, is friendly and outgoing but she has to be careful that she separates her feelings from her work. She must be objective and dispassionate while doing her work. She must maintain an 'arm's length' attitude toward her clients. She must maintain her professional standards and report based on what she finds, not what her client may say. Stories abound of auditing firms, some with very famous names who did not maintain this objectivity and sense of responsibility to the stockholders and stakeholders in carrying out their functions as an objective external auditor. Sharon's reputation and her license depend on her professional attitude.

Chapter 8 – Jobs in Accounting: Financial Accounting

Most organizations and business firms have someone in charge of the financial office. Frequently this is called the Comptroller's Office (pronounced controller) and is staffed with people educated and trained in accounting. The head of the office is frequently a CPA and directs the staff in her office as well as providing advice and counsel to the top management. This position is usually one that reports directly to the owner or owners of the firm, or to the CEO (Chief Executive Officer) and is often referred to as the CFO or Chief Financial Officer.

In the private sector, these jobs are usually challenging and of course, vital to the health of the operation. One such member of management is George Wilson. He is the CFO for a medium sized firm, Catch of the Day Restaurants, a chain of restaurants, specializing in seafood meals.

George is the head of comptrollers office and reports on the firm's financial position. He uses several important indicators, in addition to the periodic income statements. Balance sheets are updated annually since they tend to change more slowly than other reports. Here are two of the important measures, expressed as ratios.

Current Ratio is a comparison of how well the firm is prepared to meet its current obligations, and is expressed as the ratio of current assets to current liabilities.

Current Ratio

Current Assets/Current Liabilities

If an organization finds itself with a current ratio of less than unity, that means it is at risk of being illiquid to the extent that it may become bankrupt. It does not have the means to pay its current obligations. These may be payables to suppliers, wages and salaries to employees or taxes due to the government. None of these can be sustained for long periods of time.

The firm's accountants may suggest strategies such as taking on long term debt to reduce current short term debt by means of paying off important payables but there is likely to be a serious underlying problems that is causing the organization to not be able to generate revenue with its assets.

If we look back at the Income Statement for Martin Company, we can see that the Current Ratio is $31,191/$14,685 or 2.13. This indicates Martin Company has more than enough current assets to meet its current liabilities, even if it encounters difficulties in generating revenue for a short period of time.

An example of a situation in which a firm might find jeopardy is the event of a serious business interruption like a flood or fire. The liabilities will not go away just because the firm cannot operate but the current assets will shrink rapidly since there will be no revenue for a period of time. If the firm is able to get back into operation quickly, they might avert disaster. This is an instance when business interruption insurance may be a strong recommendation by the accounting department.

Another important ratio measures the efficiency of the firm, that is, how well is it doing in converting its resources into revenue and is calculated by the ratio between Operating Expenses and Operating Revenue, both of which come from the Income Statement. This is called the Operating Ratio.

> **Operating Ratio**
>
> Operating Expenses/Operating Revenue

For the Martin Company, the Operating Ratio is $26,915/$34,652 or 0.78. This number must always be less than 1 and the smaller, the better. There are two important ways to analyze this number. First, is the current level compared with the prior periods? The second is to compare, wherever possible, to similar ratios for other companies in the same industry. As standalone ratios, they do not mean much. However, for example, when the Operating Ratio gets close to 1.0 or even exceeds 1.0, the firm is in serious trouble because its operating expenses exceed its operating revenue. The Current Ratio should always be greater than 1.0, meaning that the firm can meet its current obligations and the Operating Ratio must be significantly less than 1.

George makes certain that these numbers are accurate and in fact, since Catch of the Day maintains an internal local area network for its managers, he posts these numbers on the internal system and because his software closes out each day, the top management can see these important ratios almost on a Real Time basis.

Remember that the product of accounting is information and information is valuable to management only when it is available, timely, dependable and accurate.

We will discuss these and many more indicators and ratios in a later chapter.

Chapter 9 – Tax Accounting

Almost all countries have complex tax systems, covering the range from income taxes, property taxes, tariffs on imported goods, sales taxes, value added taxes, and anything else that the governments can think of. The watchword might be "if it moves, tax it, if it doesn't move, tax it anyway." These systems can be very complex and taxes are applied at all levels of government. One of the most important services accountants perform is keeping track of the client's tax liability and making certain it is paid, on time and in the right amount.

These specialists are in demand in all countries and all industries. Not understanding and complying with the myriad tax laws can get an organization in trouble faster than almost anything else and it requires a specialist to make sure the right taxes are paid and that the client does not pay more tax than is required by law.

Tax accountants work in large and small firms, and can even be on staff for large, complex multinational CPA and Consulting organizations. Many other tax accountants are self-employed and also serve other accounting tasks for a variety of clients. Carl Waters is such a tax accountant. He operates a small accounting firm in a medium sized city in Indiana. Carl employs three people, all of whom are trained in accounting and Carl himself is a CPA.

Carl spent 12 years working for the IRS as a tax agent and then became an Enrolled Agent before he opened his own office. Enrolled Agents are certified by the IRS as qualified to advise clients on tax matters and to represent them before the IRS authorities. Because of his years with the IRS, Carl is very familiar with many industries. He decided to open his own office six years ago and has an important list of clients. He and his staff perform many accounting functions for these clients in addition to preparing tax returns and setting up the recording systems needed within the client firm to maintain the records required. He also advises clients on ways to reduce their tax liability, within the limits of the tax laws.

Chapter 10 – Accounting Consultants

Many organizations, especially large firms have a myriad of issues with which accountants must deal. Setting up accounting systems, assisting in public stock offerings, developing long-term strategic plans and so forth are tasks for which many organizations seek outside help from specialized consulting firms and many of these include large numbers of accountants.

Accountants working for these consulting firms often develop specific areas of expertise in which they provide skills that the requesting firms and organizations cannot afford to employ full time.

Many of these consulting firms offer a wide range of services including but certainly not limited to management services, marketing studies, investment counseling, stock offerings, fraud investigation (forensic accounting), human resources management and personnel development, taxes, international business matters and more.

Many of these organizations select certain industries or sectors as areas of specialization, such as aerospace and defense, automotive industries, medical management, chemical industries or public sector, to name a few.

Accountants who work in these organizations often find themselves with a variety of clients and develop specialties important to the firms. Not all of them must be accountants but in general, a study of accountancy is a common starting point.

Helen Crandall is just such an employee. She works for an internationally known consulting firm with offices in many countries. Helen's specialty in helping client firms "Go Public", that is to issue and sell stock in order to expand their funding and ownership. They may be changing from a privately held firm to one that is publicly owned.

Helen has undergraduate and graduate degrees in Law and is a member of the Bar Association in her state of Connecticut. After completing her law studies, she continued in school and earned an MBA. This qualified her to become a CPA and develop her specialty. Most of the dealings are with firms across the country but since she is so deeply involved in Wall Street, she has her office in New York City. In her work, she advises companies in how to make the change from private to public ownership.

Chapter 11 - Forensic Accounting

Harold Waterson is an FBI Agent working in the field of Forensic Accounting. He has a Bachelor's Degree in Accounting from a Midwestern state university and has completed a Master's Degree in Forensic Accounting from a well-known University. He has been with the FBI for 12 years, after completing the mandatory 20 weeks of training at the FBI facility in Quantico, Virginia. Prior to joining the FBI, he worked as an accountant for a major public accounting firm.

He works for the FBI as a Forensic Accountant, investigating a wide range of illicit activities ranging from public official corruption to money laundering and fraud. He is a CPA and belongs to the American Board of Forensic Accounting and the American Institute of CPAs.

In his job, he is required to travel all around the United States, investigating his wide range of issues. His favorite investigation involves corruption of public officials. To do so, he often has to interview the individuals involved, others in the official's office, people accused of offering bribes or whatever the specific case involves.

Harold feels very satisfied with his profession and his accomplishments. He knows that public corruption is present and causes losses to the general public and distorts the normal functioning of government.

In addition to the investigation part, he must also frequently testify in court when these suspects are tried for their crimes. Part of his FBI training helped him become comfortable in testifying as an expert witness.

Mary Kay Ryan is also a forensic accountant but she works for one of the major consulting firms. She has a Bachelor's degree in accounting and a Master's Degree in economics and she is a CPA. She belongs to the American Board of Forensic Accounting and the American Institute of CPAs.

Her job does not require nearly as much travel as others in her field and she seldom has to testify in court. Rather, she works in the corporate office in Cleveland, Ohio and spends her time reviewing records for clients who are worried about internal embezzling by employees, usually called "white collar crime".

She reports to the head of the Forensic Division of her firm and is responsible for reviewing evidence brought to her by the field agents. These agents are not necessarily forensic accountants and receive guidance from the team leader of the investigation in the field. Instead, she carefully examines the evidence and reports her findings to the team leader.

Chapter 12 - Personal Accounting

Everyone who has income and expenses needs to carry out Personal Accounting, ranging from balancing a checkbook to filing personal tax returns. These people do not have to be trained in bookkeeping or accounting but do need to keep certain records. This is part of Personal Accounting.

Other parts of personal accounting are things like keeping track of bills so they can be paid on time, establishing a budget and monitoring many other bits of information like credit card invoices, to watch for errors and unauthorized charges.

In today's atmosphere of Identity Theft, we all need to learn to work as a forensic accountant, analyzing what charges were made, by whom and working with the bank or credit card company to get these charges removed.

At other times, everyone must be tax accountants, taking action to minimize tax liabilities, keeping track of legitimate deductions and filing the return.

Chapter 13 – Measures and Ratios

The product of accounting is information. This chapter examines the form and determination of the important information accountants need to produce and report to management, owners, stakeholders and stockholders. The Comptroller's Office has the responsibility of setting up the recording, analysis and reporting structures to keep management informed of the condition of the organization, giving warnings and counsel to management in advance of issues to prevent adverse situations.

To do so, the CFO will use two types of strategies for extracting important information; static and dynamic. Static analysis measures various important signals at some point in time, for example, the current ration as described earlier. These are measures taken at some point in time, to assess the current situation. Dynamic analyses are those that examine the organization's performance over some period of time, like month-to-month or year over year. These dynamic analyses provide important trend analysis, allowing some prediction of future performance under these same conditions. That means 'here is what will be in the future if we don't make a change.'

These measures are taken from both the Balance Sheet and from the Income Statement, depending upon the model needed. These measures can be grouped into three categories; measures of financial strength, operating efficiency and organization profitability. See Appendix 1 for illustrations of many of these measures and ratios.

Financial Strength

Long Term Financial Strength:

An organization must be able to withstand the normal and sometimes worse than normal vicissitudes of its life. It must be in a position of strength to maintain its ability to carry out its chosen mission, whether that mission is manufacturing, extraction, service or distribution. The many stakeholders and stockholders expect that management will be capable of guiding the firm through the perils of everyday business life without failing or going out of business. The organization must be resilient and able to maintain its forward progress under any reasonably expected events.

Here are some commonly used measures of financial strength:

Equity to Liabilities Ratio:

$$\frac{\text{Owner's Equity}}{\text{Total Liabilities}}$$

Remember that all assets of the organization must come from either inside the operation or by borrowing from outside. This ratio shows the source of the assets as a proportion from the Owner's Equity and from all Liabilities, including Current Liabilities. In modern terms, "How much skin do the owners have in the game?" A low ratio indicates that most of the assets come from outside the organization, not from the owners. A higher ratio, approaching unity would indicate a solidly built firm with good grounding by the owners. Too low a ratio might indicate high levels of borrowing or high levels of current liabilities. Too high a ratio might indicate the opportunity to leverage the assets by increasing outside funding from sources such as long-term loans or bonds.

Times Interest Earned:

$$\text{Net Income Before Interest and Taxes} / \text{Total Interest Payments}$$

Whatever leverage strategy the organization chooses, it must pay the interest on outstanding loans, both short term and long term. The holders of this debt want assurance that the organization can earn enough to pay the interest owed on a timely basis. This ratio captures that ability. A low number indicates risk for the lenders, a higher number of times interest earned is an indication of safety.

Debt to Equity Ratio:

The Debt to Equity Ratio measures the degree to which the organization is leveraged, between assets and debt. This is particularly informative for long-term debt, since short-term debt like accounts payable is usually very fluid and is not a useful source of operating capital.

> **Total Debt (Current and Long Term)/Total Equity**

Together, these three ratios can show the strength of the firm in terms of its ability to meet its obligations and the extent to which the owners have contributed to that strength.

Short Term Financial Strength:

Current Ratio:

As described earlier, the Current Ratio tells us how well the firm is prepared to meet its current obligations, and is expressed as the ratio of current assets to current liabilities.

> **Current Assets/Current Liabilities**

This ratio is one with two edges; a larger number indicates good assurance of meeting current liabilities, i.e. the organization is very capable of meeting its short-term obligations. However, too large a ratio might indicate that current assets, like cash and cash equivalents are being held in preference to being put to work earning profits.

Quick Ratio:

The Quick Ratio is a bit more severe than the Current Ratio because is compares only the total of cash and accounts receivable with current liabilities. This leaves out the value of the inventory and prepaids and is regarded as a better assessment of strength in the immediate sense. This ratio is sometimes called the Acid Test. It does represent the availability if immediate action to resolve Current Liabilities is needed.

> **(Cash + AccountsReceivable)/Current Liabilities**

Operating Efficiency

Measures of Operating Efficiency tell management how well and effectively they are using the assets they have. These are easy calculations but are very useful as a static measure and for watching trends over time as dynamic analyses.

Receivables Turnover:

The Receivables Turnover Ratio indicates how efficient the organization is at collecting money due from customers. Like the others, this is an easy calculation and these results should be available at request from the accounting system. This ratio should be as low as possible, indicating prompt payment by customers.

> **Net Sales/ Average Accounts Receivable**

Inventory Turnover:

Inventory is an asset in which the organization has chosen to invest. In practice, investments in inventory represent opportunities lost to invest in more productive assets and should be minimized with a well-planned material control system. Keeping track of Inventory Turnover is important for an operation trying to apply concepts of Lean Management.

> **Cost of Goods Sold/Average Inventory**

Turnover of Assets:

Like receivables and inventory, assets are investment choices by the organization's management. This measure is not too common but is informative. It shows how well the management is employing the assets is holds. It reveals how many times the total assets are being used in the firm's operation.

> **Total Sales/Average Total Assets**

Operating Ratio:

The operating ratio shows how much of each unit of revenue is consumed by operating expense, and how much is left over to contribute to the firm's profits.

> **Operating Expense/Operating Revenue**

Profitability

One of the most important indicators for management and outside stakeholders are the measures of profitability.

Profit Margin:

This may be the most recognized measure of the profitability of the organization and is a widely used measure. It is usually expressed as a percentage. This is often referred to as Return on Sales or ROS.

It is frequently used in one of two forms, the second being a little more restrictive in that it eliminates any revenue from sources other than operations.

> **Net Income/Total Revenues**
> **Net Operating Income/Total Sales**

Return on Investment:

Return on Investment or ROI or Return on Assets (ROA) is another very commonly used measure of the profitability of a firm. The individual accounting analyst may choose whether to use Average Total Assets and Net Income Before Taxes and Interest or some other shading that may suit the needs of the firm better. For example, the analyst may choose to exclude other income such as interest, rents and royalties and restrict this measure only to operations.

> **Net Income Before Taxes and Interest/Total Assets**

Return on Equity:

A similar measure examines the equity of the owners, for a privately held organization, total owner's equity or for a publicly held organization, total stock equity. Again, the details should be left to the management as to exactly how to compute Return on Equity or ROE.

> **Net Income Before Taxes and Interest/Total Equity**

Return on Capital Employed

This ratio, often called ROCE, measures how efficiently the firm uses its capital investment to earn profits. The ratio is shown below.

> $$\frac{\text{Profit before Interest and Taxes}}{\text{Total Assets} - \text{Current Liabilities}}$$

Chapter 14 – Accounting Software

For all but the smallest organizations, accounting software is essential to an effective financial control system. Individuals selling items on the internet for example, may be able to keep the necessary records manually, in hard copy on paper or a computer spreadsheet, but the image of old time accountants sitting at a wooden desk wearing green eyeshades and working with an ink pen, is interesting history but today's world requires much better systems. Think of Charles Dickens' characters Ebenezer Scrooge and Bob Cratchet.

When an organization, whether for profit or not-for-profit, has more than one individual with responsibilities, a real accounting system is needed and the larger the organization, the greater the need for a computer based system.

The simplest of these may be ones like QuickBooks®, SAGE 50®, XERO® or WAVE®, useful for small to medium size businesses. An advantage of several of these is that no accounting training is needed to set them up and operate them. They all tend to be very intuitive.

Larger organizations needing more comprehensive accounting packages have a wide variety from which to select. These more complex systems usually require specialized training available from the software vendors.

A few characteristics are common to all packages. First, they should be designed with easy to use graphical interfaces, intuitive command structures and system design. They should be capable of producing the common accounting reports using the well-known ratios, percentages and rates common to all accounting systems. They should also be able to generate such reports on demand and to track progress of this information over time for trend analyses.

Many are adaptable to integrated data management ranging from order entry, invoicing, shipping data, inventory recording and control, accounts payable management and payroll processing, to name just a few. Some go as far as ERP or Enterprise Resources Planning, which includes a number of extra features that integrate some, most or all of the "back office" functions into a single platform. These functions can include product and production planning, scheduling, materials planning and purchasing, inventory control, distribution, accounting, and even many human resources functions like payroll. These systems are complex but are becoming essential for large organizations and enterprises. The emphasis is on the enterprise; the total operation whether it is manufacturing, retailing, finance, or not for profit operations and foundations.

Some complex systems can automate the ordering, receiving, payment functions, payroll records and check writing, and many others that are frequently done manually.

One important feature all systems should be to provide automatic generation of the various ratios and measures discussed in the previous chapter, both instantaneously and with trend analysis. Systems that are more sophisticated allow managers to examine the trends in these ratios and indicators from their own desk, as desired.

Chapter 15 - Time Value of Money - Present Value Concepts

One very fundamental concept in accounting, personal life and business in general is that of the Time Value of Money. We all would prefer money today rather than the promise of money in the future. Businesses, however, do not always have the cash available to make critical investments when needed. They may need to borrow the funds in order to make the investment, which is intended to increase the revenue or decrease costs.

We all recognize that there is a relationship between time and the value of money. That relationship is mathematically modeled with the concept of present value. This is not a difficult concept to understand and compute but for complex cases, the manual computation is time consuming and can lead to errors. Fortunately, computer spreadsheet programs can do all of the computations for us. We just need to properly understand and describe the problem in correct terms.

The basic notion of Present Value is that the value of something sometime in the future is not as great as its value today. Economists, engineers and accountants model this difference mathematically through the various equations to calculate present value. For example, an investment in a new machine may reduce manufacturing costs, but the firm must pay for the new machine. It will generate a series of annual cost savings that have some present value. In order to evaluate this project, we use Present Value mathematics. (See the example with Modern Manufacturing below.)

To accomplish that, we will introduce some new definitions. For several of these, we will provide illustrations.

Present Value (P); the value of an asset now, today or the amount of investment proposed.

The present value of a $100 bill is $100. The present value of a new machine proposed to be purchased is the amount of money to acquire, deliver and install the machine.

Future Value (F); the value of an asset at some selected time in the future, which may be expressed in days, months or even years. If we have some positive interest rate, this will be larger than the present value.

An amount of money deposited in a Certificate of Deposit at 5% annual interest will have a future value larger than the original deposit depending upon the amount deposited and the number of years left on deposit. Thus, for an amount of $1000 at 5% annual interest will be worth $1050 at the end of one year.

Interest Rate (i); the rate, which is associated with the passage of time for a specified asset. This may be for example, the interest charged on a credit card by the card issuer or the rate paid by an investment like a certificate of deposit. **The interest rate is the relationship between time and money**.

Number of Time Periods (n); the number of periods being considered, for example 24 months, 5 years, and so forth. The time period must agree with the interest rate. If the period is 1 month, the interest rate must be expressed as rate per month. This is extremely important since in the computation, if this rule is not followed, the output will be false.

Periodic Payment (A); for a case in which the payments are made periodically, this represents the number of payments to be made. These may be monthly, annually or whatever is consistent with n and i, or the periodic savings resulting from an investment.

Net Present Value (NPV); this is the present value of an investment made with periodic returns (A) at a specified interest rate and number of periods minus the amount of the investment to acquire the asset.

Here are some examples of the decisions made based on the Present Value model.

Modern Manufacturing has the opportunity to install automation that will have the effect of reducing labor costs by $25,000 per year. This amount was determined by the engineers and the CFO is confident it is accurate. The automation will cost $55,000 to acquire, install and launch. They expect it to last at least 8 years. To evaluate this project, we need to determine the net present value (NPV) for this project. If the NPV is positive, we will save that amount of money over the eight-year period. Remember that NPV accounts for the investment as well as the resulting savings.

We regard the P value for the project to be $55,000, with $25,000 as the value for A, the periodic return and the firm uses an interest rate of 14% to evaluate these projects.

We enter an Excel® spreadsheet with those values and determine the NPV to be $57,082. That is determined by accounting for the i = 0.14, 8 annual savings of $25,000 each and the initial investment of $55,000, using an Excel® spreadsheet. The Present Value of this savings stream is $112,082. By subtracting the initial investment of $55,000, we arrive at the Net Present Value, $57,082.

Therefore, the decision to make the investment is a good one. However, this decision must be compared with any other projects that are competing for the organization's capital funds, and any other considerations not included such as effects on productivity.

This is important because very few if any organizations have sufficient capital resources to take advantage of all their opportunities. Present value considerations are an important tool for organizations to decide how to deploy scarce assets.

Cost of Capital

As we have seen in the three important documents; i.e. the Balance Sheet, the Income Statement and the Cash Flow Statement, we need to invest money to improve and expand our business. We may borrow that money from external lenders in the form of loans, mortgages or bonds. We will have to pay for those funds at some agreed upon interest rate.

Alternatively, we could sell stock in the firm to raise capital. When we do that, our investors will expect a return for letting us use their money, so we may have to pay dividends to the stockholders.

Our third alternative is to have the owners invest more money, but again, our owners will expect a return on their investment. Money is never free, unless we generate it through profits, and we may need to invest in assets in order to generate more profits.

Cost of Capital is the cost that the firm has to pay to get the capital it uses. This is applies to both equity and debt capital and includes interest, dividends and payments for preferred stocks as well as returns to owners.

Determining the cost of these alternatives is important and we term that cost the "Cost of Capital." Mathematically, cost of capital is the weighted average of all our sources of funds, from owners, lenders or stockholders.

Example using Modern Manufacturing

Modern Manufacturing is a publicly owned company whose stock is traded on the New York Stock Exchange. The stock is currently valued at $22. Modern pays an annual dividend of $1.50 for a rate of 3.3 percent at the current share price. There are currently 50,000 shares outstanding.

They have an outstanding long-term loan of $4,000,000 at an interest rate of 8% and for new investments, they are paying 9.5% interest. They do not plan to borrow more at this time.

The founders of the firm hold Preferred Stock shares, which pay a dividend of 6%, and there are 45,000 shares outstanding at a current price of $75.

Source	Total Amount ($000's)	Percentage	Annual Cost ($000's)
Common Stock	1,100.	3.3%	36.3
Preferred Stock	1,650	6%	99.
Loans	4,000	8%	320.
Total Funding	6,750		455.3
Weighted Average Cost of Capital		6.75%	

This analysis tells us that the weighted average cost of capital is 6.75%. That means that any discretionary investment must pay back at least that amount. In order to provide a floor for new capital investments the management has set a minimum rate or hurdle rate of 14%. Any proposed capital project must be discounted at the hurdle rate. Modern Manufacturing has chosen 14% as their minimum IRR. Any project which does not meet or exceed this rate will not be approved.

Internal Rate of Return

Another way to look at these decisions is to determine the discount rate which makes the NPV equal to zero. This is called the "Internal Rate of Return" or IRR. This rate must be greater than the cost of capital and the higher the better. IRR is commonly used to compare projects that are competing for the scarce capital funds. Internal rate of return computations are not simple but fortunately, spreadsheet programs can compute it directly. IRR is presently the strongest means to evaluate capital projects. However, this is true for discretionary investments. If an investment must be made because of some situation for which the firm has no choice, such as regulatory compliance or safety issues, the firm will work hard to engineer the least expensive solution and will accept whatever IRR is determined.

Payback Period

Payback Period is another, simpler way to look at investments. It ignores the time value concept. It just looks at the investment, and determines how long it will take to pay back the investment.

Using the example above for Modern Manufacturing, the total amount to be saved over the 8 years is 8*$25,000 or $200,000. Based on an investment of $55,000, the investment will be paid back in 3.64 years. We can see that in terms of present value, the payback method overstates the present value of the investment by nearly $90,000. ($200,000 - 112,082 = $87918.) This clearly demonstrates the importance of considering present value considerations in making these decisions.

Conclusion

Our objective in this book was to introduce readers who are not accountants to the fundamental concepts and vocabulary of the world of accounting.

We have explained that the product of accounting is information. Information is needed by owners, managers, supervisors, employees, investors and all the other stakeholders. The various regulatory and taxing authorities are important members of this group of stakeholders.

A number of accounting positions are described along with the education and training required for them.

We have explained and discussed the three important reports produced by the accounting office; the Income Statement, the Balance Sheet and the Cash Flow Statement. The examples for these reports and statements illustrate their important contents.

Further, we have introduced some commonly used methods to evaluate the information reported, in terms of position, income, efficiency and strength for the organization. Appendix 1 includes an example case with the results for many of these ratios and measures.

We trust that this book has met your expectations. It was not intended to make the reader an accountant but rather, to introduce the profession and practice of accounting and point out how management and other stakeholders use this information for planning and decision making.

Appendix 1

Barksdale Construction is a large developer of commercial and residential properties. The owners invested $250,000 to start the company a number of years ago and then expanded their financing by selling preferred stock at an 8% dividend rate. This means that Preferred Dividends must be paid before any other payments from earnings, that is the preferred stockholders have priority over the other owners. The company has not sold any common stock so it is not considered publicly owned.

The last section contains several commonly used ratios and measures for Barksdale Construction. No judgment is made since these measures are most important when compared with budget, prior periods and common industry results. Interested parties will use these results to draw judgments about the firm and compare these results with similar firms in the same industry.

BALANCE SHEET

BARKSDALE CONSTRUCTION COMPANY, INC.

Asset/Liability	$	$
Current Assets		
Cash and Marketable Securities	180,000	
Accounts Receivable	43,000	
Inventories	125,000	
Total Current Assets		348,000
Land and Buildings	248,000	
Equipment	310,000	
Accumulated Depreciation	105,000	
Investments and Undeveloped Property	540,000	
Intangibles	16,000	
Total Long Term Assets		1,219,000
Total Assets		1,567,000
Liabilities		
Accounts Payable	25,000	
Taxes Payable	15,000	
Dividends Payable	14,000	
Total Current Liabilities		54,000
Preferred Stock	674,000	
Notes Payable	180,000	
Mortgages Payable	252,000	
Invested Capital	250,000	
Retained Earnings	157,000	
Total Owners Equity		1,513,000
Total Liabilities and Equity		1,567,000

INCOME STATEMENT

BARKSDALE CONSTRUCTION COMPANY, INC.

Year Ended December 31, 2015

Revenue/Disbursements	$	$
Sales	2,368,500	
Less Uncollectibles	(5,280)	
Gross Revenue	2,363,220	
Operating Expenses		
Cost of Goods Sold	1,368,000	
Wages and Salaries	357,370	
Supplies Expense	2,895	
Insurance Premiums	23,000	
Depreciation Expense	35,400	
General and Administrative	37,890	
Property Taxes	48,750	
Total Operating Expenses	1,837,905	
Operating Profit	525,315	
Other Expenses		
Dividends Paid	24,500	
Interest Expense	2,470	
Profit Before Taxes	498,345	
Income Taxes	174,421	
Net Profit	498,345	

Measures and Ratios for Barksdale Construction Company

Equity to Liability Ratio	$461,000/$1,567,000 = 0.30
Times Interest Earned	$525,315/$26,970 = 19.48
Debt to Equity Ratio	$1,160,000/$407,000 = 2.85
Current Ratio	$348,000/$54,000 = 6.45
Receivables Turnover	$2,363,220/$1,219,000 = 54.96
Turnover of Assets	$2,363,220/$$1,219,000 = 1.94
Operating Ratio	$1,802,505/$$2,363,220 = 0.77
Return on Investment (ROI)	$560,715/$1,567,000 = 41%
Return on Equity (ROE)	$560,715/$1,513,000 = 37%
Return on Capital Employed (ROCE)	$560,715/$1,513,000 = 37%

Part 3: Accounting

An Essential Guide to Learning Accounting Quickly

Introduction

How many times have we shunned away from accounting? What many of us do not realize is that accounting is in our day-to-day lives and we do not even realize it.

If you have ever balanced a checkbook or kept a ledger for your bank accounts then you are performing some kind of accounting operation.

We are going to expand on those simple tasks by showing how they relate to accounting. Then we will build on that and introduce you to accounting.

Accounting is not just for businesses. As you will see, it is for all of us, every day of our lives. Imagine if you want to buy a house. You need to figure out mortgage payments, interests, etc. Those estimates that both you and the bank perform is accounting. The same goes for buying a car or renting an apartment.

Throughout this learning experience or journey into accounting you will learn about the guidelines for accounting that need to be followed. You will also learn many parts of the basics to help get you started.

However, as a special bonus we will take a brief look into financial analysis by showing you the five main categories of financial ratios. These ratios will help you not only with accounting analysis but also with your everyday investments. These ratios are the same ones that banks use to approve loans or businesses use to find out where their business is financially.

Take the time to absorb this information as it will help you in your everyday life and in your business ventures.

Chapter 1 – Generally Accepted Accounting Principles (GAAP)

To really understand accounting, you need to understand the rules or regulations behind it. These are also known as the standards. Overall these standards are known as the Generally Accepted Accounting Principles or GAAP.

The standards were established and developed by the Financial Accounting Foundation's (FAF) standard-setting board. This board is divided into the Financial Accounting Standards Board (FASB) and the Governmental Accounting Standards Board (GASB).

These standards regulate the language for financial reporting. In turn it communicates the financial conditions and operational results. This includes companies, both public and private, not-for-profit organizations, and state or local governments.

Financial reporting mainly includes information on the following:

- Financial position, which includes balance sheet and statement of net position
- Results of operations, which includes statement of revenues, expenses, and changes in net position
- Disclosures.

GAAP is used for providing useful information for investors, lenders, or others who need to know this information about a company. It also establishes concepts, objectives, standards, and conventions which evolve over time to guide how the statements are prepared and presented.

The principles of the GAAP include:

- Recognition—this includes items that should be recognized in a financial statement, such as assets, liabilities, revenues, and expenses.

- Measurement—this is the elements of the amounts that are included in the financial statements.

- Presentation—on the financial statements it includes the line items, subtotals, and totals. This is how that information will be displayed.

- Disclosure—this explains and supplements the amounts on the statements. It also shows specific information based on what is most important to the user.

Financial Accounting Foundation (FAF)

The FAF is the independent, private-sector, not-for-profit organization based in Norwalk, Connecticut. They are responsible for the oversight, administration, financing, and appointment of the Financial Accounting Standards Board and the Governmental Accounting Standards Board.

- Financial Accounting Standards Board (FASB)—they establish financial reporting and accounting standards for companies, both private and public. This also applies to not-for-profit organizations.

- Governmental Accounting Standards Board (GASB)—they do the same as the FASB only on a government level with the U.S., state, and local governments.

The GAAP has always been a high-quality organization of financial reporting. That way investors, lenders, capital providers, and others who need access to this information can get it. The FASB and GASB are responsible for the GAAP to continue to have those high standards.

There are many organizations that rely on this information. Today even you, as a taxpayer, are following these same standards. Others who are following the standards set by the GAAP are holders of municipal bonds, members of citizen groups, legislators, and oversight bodies. Everyone needs to look into the financial information to make good investments.

The missions of these organizations are accomplished through a pretty comprehensive and independent due process. This process encourages board participation. It also allows to objectively consider all the stakeholder views and will be subject to oversight by the FAF's Board of Trustees.

The FASB and GASB use the following steps for due process:

1. Identify Topic—the board identifies a financial reporting issue that needs to be addressed. This is based on recommendations from stakeholders, staff research, board members' concerns, or other means.

2. Conduct Pre-agenda Research—research is conducted on those issues that need to be presented.

3. Make Agenda Decision—board adds projects or concerns to be discussed at public meeting.

4. Deliberate at Public Meeting—Public meeting is held to discuss the issues and concerns.

5. Issue Document for Public Comment—the Board drafts a proposal and makes it public for comments on the proposal.

6. Host Public Hearing or Round Tables (Major Projects)—on major issues a public hearing may be called to give stakeholders a chance to comment on the issues.

7. Re-deliberate Based on Comments and Research—another meeting is held to review the comments given by the public and stakeholders.

8. Issue Final Standard—the Board issues the final paperwork with the new standards.

9. Education—the Board ensures that everyone is educated on the new standards.

10. Implementation—the new standards are now implemented.

If the standards are significant and have been in place for two or three years by GASB standards it could be selected by the FAF's Post-Implementation Review team. This team will evaluate it for its effectiveness.

What are the Qualities of the GAAP?

All businesses, regardless if you are a company, not-for-profit, or government, use standards in accounting to provide information used on financial statements. The information they need to provide is financing, lending or donating money, or determining how public officials are spending our tax money.

When a company uses financial statements that follow GAAP standards then investors and others trust that company.

The efficient, robust capital market is like one big circle.

High Quality Standards > Better Information > Greater Transparency > Better Financing Decisions > Increased Investor Confidence > High Quality Standards …

Chapter 2 – The Accounting Equation

Before we can really get into accounting, we need to first understand the accounting equation and why it is so important. If you own a business, no matter how big or small, it is the accounting equation that comes into play.

The importance of this equation is to help a company understand their financial position. By knowing this information, you can make business decisions that will help move the company forward.

Let's take a look at what is measured with the financial position of a company:

1. Assets (what a company owns)—these are the resources that the company owns. Some examples are: cash, accounts receivable, inventory, prepaid insurance, investments, land, buildings, and equipment.

2. Liabilities (what a company owes to others)—these are the obligations a company has to others. Some examples are: notes payable, loans payable, accounts payable, salaries and wages payable, interest payable, and income taxes payable.

3. Owner's equity (the difference between assets and liabilities)—these are investments into the company. It also includes net income that has not been taken from the company.

Let's take these three and put them into an equation:

- Assets = Liabilities + Owner's Equity (sole proprietorship)
- Assets = Liabilities + Stockholders' Equity (corporation)

These equations are known as the accounting equation. Each area of the equation has a purpose. The accounting equation is easy to understand and I will show you how as we continue through this book. Although, this is not the only equation that you will be faced with. More will be introduced to you as we progress through the steps.

As long as the company keeps accurate records then the equation will always be balanced. For example, if you have $1,000 in assets, $300 in liabilities, and $700 in owner's equity, then the equation is free from errors in the books. This is because you are working with double-entry accounting. We will get more into double-entry accounting in a later chapter. To simplify things let's put those numbers into the equation.

- $1,000 (assets) = $300 (liabilities) + $700 (owner's equity)

As you can see both sides of the equals must match. It is always a good idea to check the equation often. This way if the equation does not equal and there are errors you do not need to go very far back looking for errors. In the case that you find errors you would need to find out where that error is. We will cover more on this in a later chapter that will help with finding and fixing those errors.

Each transaction will be recorded in a general ledger. In turn these transactions will be on the balance sheet and the income statements. Both of these show the accounting equation.

The balance sheet is also known as the statement of financial position. This is the best report that shows the accounting equation. It will also show the company's financial position at any given time. It will report the company's assets, liabilities, and owner's equity. This report will give the totals of each area. With those totals you could use the accounting equation to find out if it is balanced. You can run this report at any time. However, most companies run it at the end of the month or quarter.

While the balance sheet reports only one point in time the income statement can cover periods of time. The income statement focuses on a company's revenue and expenses. This gives owners and stockholders an idea of where their investments are going in the company.

Chapter 3 – Cash Method Vs Accrual Method

I am sure you have heard of the cash and accrual methods in accounting. What would you use for your business? Most of the time you will only see the cash method in accounting used by small businesses, whereas the large corporations would use the accrual method. The main difference between the two is pretty simple. It is all in the timing of when revenue and expenses are recognized. Both methods are okay to use and will give you the same results.

The accrual method is the most commonly used method with business. Also, when filing your taxes, you would need to select the method that was used the first time you filed. After that you would need to file with that method each time you file your taxes.

The cash method accounts for revenue only when money is received. It also only accounts for expenses when money is paid out. However, the accrual method accounts for revenue as it is earned and expenses as they occur.

Let's make this a little simpler. We are only going to focus on the income. If you record cash or a check as it is actually received then you are using the cash method. When you record expenses as they are actually paid then you are using the cash method. If you record money coming in when you invoiced your client then you are using the accrual method. If you record expenses when you received the invoice then you are using the accrual method.

Cash Method:

- Record income when cash or check is received
- Record expense when the expense is paid

Accrual Method:

- Record income as the customer is invoiced
- Record expenses as the business is invoiced

With the accrual method you will have an account receivable and an account payable. With the cash method you will record them directly into the cash and expense accounts.

Let's take a look into Joe's purchase and we will use both methods to show how it would be recorded. Joe bought a new laser printer in April and paid $2,000 for it in June. This is two months later. Using the cash method, you would record a $2,000 payment for June. This is because that is when it was paid for. Now if you were using the accrual method, you would record the $2,000 in May. This is when you obtained the printer and agreed to pay for it.

The most significant way a business is affected by the type of method that is used is involved in the tax year. This is in part because of when particular expenses occur and are counted.

Let's take a look at another example. My friend Al runs a small candy shop called Sweet Tooth. On December 24, 2015, Al buys a new candy display case for his shop for which he was billed $250. He installed the display case that day, but according to the terms of the purchase does not pay for it for 20 days. Under his accrual system of accounting, he counts the $250 expense during the December 2015 accounting period, even though he did not actually write the check until January 2016 of the next year. This means that Al can deduct the $250 from his taxable income of 2015.

The same goes for earning income. Under the accrual method, if you finished the job and earned the income in December 2014 but did not receive payment until February of 2015 you would still need to report it as income on your 2014 taxes.

As you can see it does not matter which method you choose, you will get the same results. The only time it would give a different result is if you purchased on credit. However, in the end you will still receive the same results.

By now you are probably asking yourself which would be the best to use for your company or business. Let me help with that decision a little. If you have sales less than $5 million per year, most businesses are free to choose which method to adopt or use for their business. Although, keep this in mind: if your business has an inventory of items that you sell to the public then IRS requires you to use the accrual method. Inventory would include any merchandise you sell and includes supplies for items that will be intended to sell to the public.

As you can see both methods will give you the same results. However, they both only show a partial picture of your financial status, only in different ways.

When you use the accrual method it will show the flow of business income and debts more accurately. However, you would not know what cash reserves are available. This will result in a serious cash flow problem. For example, your income ledger may show hundreds of dollars in sales. But you bank account is empty as you are waiting for payments from customers.

Now let's look at the cash method. It gives you a much clearer picture of how much cash your business has; however, it may offer a misleading picture of longer-term profitability. For example, your ledger shows one month being very profitable although your sales have been slow. Also, you have a lot of customers who paid on credit who paid their bills that month.

To truly understand your business financial standpoint, you need more than just numbers and totals. You need answers to financial questions so that you know where your money is going and coming from.

Chapter 4 – Double-Entry Accounting

Double-entry accounting is really where you learn how to record your numbers and where to put them. Before we get talking about this form of accounting we need to mention the chart of accounts. The chart of accounts is a document that lists the name of each account and account number in the company.

For example, if you have cash, accounts receivable, accounts payable, capital, and supplies expense as your accounts your chart of accounts may look like this:

Assets:

Cash: 100

Accounts Receivable: 130

Liabilities:

Accounts Payable: 200

Supplies Expense: 230

Owner's Equity:

Joe Stern, capital: 300

Now that we have an idea about the chart of accounts I want you to look at the transactions that will be recorded for your company. Every transaction is recorded in a journal. This is the book of the original transactions. These transactions will either increase or decrease your company's accounts. These entries consist of the date of the transaction, the names of each account that is affected, reference number, and the amount of each transaction. All this information will be coming from the various source documents. For example, invoices would be considered a source document.

From the journal we will record each of these transactions into the general ledger. The general ledger is a summary of the balances of all accounts used by your company. It will have a separate journal for each account in the chart of accounts. This will have the name of the individual account and the account number at the top of the journal. The account number will be the reference number in the journal. Then the journal for the general ledger will consist of the date, description, and amounts. Then we transfer the amounts over to the general ledger; we call it posting. You would not record the reference number on the main journal until you post it to the general ledger. This helps keep track of the accounts that you have already posted and you are better organized as to where it was posted.

A good way to look at it is when you balance your bank account or your checkbook. The ledger that you record your transactions on will be a journal. When you compare it to your statements then you will check that it is posted correctly. Also, this will have two columns for your amounts. It will either be debit and credit or deposit and withdrawal. This is a form of the double-entry accounting for recording journal entries.

Debits and Credits

With double-entry accounting, every transaction made will have at least two entries: a debit and a credit. Most of us think that a debit decreases our account and a credit increases our account. When recording the entries in your journal for your bank account this is true. Mainly because you are only working with cash in and cash out of your account. In accounting the debit means left and the credit means right. This is because depending on what is being recorded a debit could either increase or decrease the account. The same for credits. The following will show if debits and credits will increase or decrease the accounts.

ACCOUNT	DEBIT (Left side)	CREDIT (Right Side)
Assets	Increase	Decrease
Liabilities	Decrease	Increase
Owner's Equity	Decrease	Increase
Revenue	Decrease	Increase
Expenses	Increase	Decrease

There are several steps that need to be taken when entering debits and credits into the journal. These steps will make up a journal entry and will be repeated for each entry made.

1. We need to figure out which accounts will be affected by the transaction.
2. Once the affected accounts are decided, then you need to find out whether this account will increase or decrease the account.
3. Every time you make a transaction both the debits and credits will equal. Sometimes you will have multiple transactions as the credit or debit depending on what accounts need to be affected.
4. Always list the account that will be debited first and will be on the left side. Then you will indent the credits so that they will show on the right side.
5. Ensure that the debits and credits are recorded on the correct side and that they equal.

T Accounts

To simplify things let's look at them as T accounts. Each account type will have either a debit normal balance or a credit normal balance. The following information will help you in knowing which account has a debit or a credit normal balance.

- ASSETS—Debit Normal Balance
- LIABILITIES—Credit Normal Balance
- OWNER'S CAPITAL—Credit Normal Balance
- OWNER'S DRAWING—Debit Normal Balance
- REVENUE—Credit Normal Balance
- EXPENSES—Debit Normal Balance

These are considered the five major accounts—assets, liabilities, owner's equity, revenues, and expenses.

Assets		Liabilities		Owner's Capital	
Debit	Credit	Debit	Credit	Debit	Credit
Increase	Decrease	Decrease	Increase	Decrease	Increase
Normal Bal			Normal Bal		Normal Bal

Owner's Drawing		Revenue		Expenses	
Debit	Credit	Debit	Credit	Debit	Credit
Increase	Decrease	Decrease	Increase	Decrease	Increase
Normal Bal			Normal Bal	Normal Bal	

T accounts are only a part of the journaling process. It makes it easy to put in perspective if each account is to be debited or credited based on if it is to be increased or decreased.

Keep in mind as you begin working with the closing entries and the reports, it is important to know which accounts are affected, whether you will increase the account or decrease the account, whether it will be a debit or a credit that will increase that account, and whether the account will have a debit normal balance or a credit normal balance.

This information will help you as you start to prepare the worksheet, the income statements, the trial balance, the statement of retained earnings, the statement of owner's equity, the cash flow statement, and many other reports that will help show a bigger picture of the company's status.

Chapter 5 – Financial Statements

Trial Balance

Once you have posted all transactions and now have all your balances calculated you can prepare the trial balance. The trial balance is a document that lists all your assets, liabilities, owner's equity, revenue, and expenses. It also allows us to verify that all the debits and credits equal.

This can be prepared at any given time. However, most of the time it is prepared at the end of a specific period, for instance, at the end of a month, quarter, or year. If ever in doubt of your debits and credits equaling you can prepare a trial balance.

Income Statement

The first document is the income statement. This statement will show a company's net income or net loss for a specific period; that is, it will show the company's worth after all revenues and expenses are accounted for.

The heading of the income statement will always list the company's name, statement name, and accounting period. There are three columns on this statement.

1. List all revenue accounts followed by all expense accounts.
2. All expense account totals or the debit column. If you remember previously, expenses have a debit normal balance.
3. List revenue account totals or the credit column. If you remember previously, revenue has a credit normal balance.

Remember this equation for the income statement:

- Revenue – Expenses = Net Income or Net Loss

Income Statement

ABC Financial Company, Inc.

For the Month Ending July 31

REVENUES

Service revenue: $13,000

Interest revenue: $400

Total revenue: $13,400

EXPENSES

Office supplies expense: $2,000

Salaries expense: $2,120

Rent expense: $1,000

Total expenses: $5,120

Net income: $8,800

Statement of Retained Earnings

Once the income statement is prepared you will want to prepare a statement of retained earnings. This statement will show where your company is at the end of the given month. As the retained earnings are carried over from the previous month then we will add the earnings for the current month so that we will see where we stand at the end of the month. In turn these earnings will be carried over the next month's retained earnings statement.

Retained Earnings Statement

ABC Financial Company, Inc.

For the Month Ending July 31

Retained earnings as of July 1: $2,450

Net income: $8,800

Total: $11,250

Less dividends: ($400)

Retained earnings ending balance: $10,850

As you can see the income statement provides some valuable information. This is where you will be able to get a good look at what you are bringing in as a company after all the expenses have been paid and accounted for.

The Balance Sheet

The final document to prepare from the trial balance is the balance sheet. This is a list of all your assets, liabilities, and owner's equity accounts, as well as the balances of these accounts on a specific date. The easiest way to remember this is that it is simply a detailed version of the accounting equation.

Assets = Liabilities + Owner's Equity

ASSETS	=	LIABILITIES	+	OWNER'S EQUITY
Cash		Accounts payable		Revenues
Accounts receivable				Expenses
Supplies				Drawing accounts
Equipment				

The chart above will give you an idea of the balance sheet. The first thing you will have is the heading. This will include the report name, the company name, and the date it was prepared for.

Next you will list all your assets with the totals of each one. You will then total all your assets. Next you will list all your liabilities as well as their totals. Finally, you will list all your owner's equity along with their totals. Lastly, take the totals of the liabilities plus the owner's equity. This total should equal that of the assets. See the example below.

Balance Sheet

ABC Financial Company, Inc.

July 31

ASSETS

Cash: $9,000

Accounts receivable: $2,000

Materials: $4,000

Equipment: $5,500

Total assets: $20,500

LIABILITIES AND OWNER'S EQUITY

Liabilities

Accounts payable: $1,750

Salaries payable: $7,000

Total liabilities: $8,750

Owner's equity (retained earnings): $11,750

Total liabilities and owner's equity: $20,500

Chapter 6 – Making Adjusting Entries

As we go along with making our transactions you will find that you will need to make some adjustment entries. In the accrual-based accounting you will make adjusting entries to make sure that the correct amounts are recorded for the revenue and expense transactions.

Prepaid Expense

The first of these entries will be prepaid expenses. This is a cost that is paid for before it has actually happened. They provide a short-term benefit to the company and so can be considered as a current asset. For example, if you paid your rent for eight months you would have the benefit of not needing to pay your rent for that time. An adjustment would be made each month to show that the rent has incurred for that time. Every time a part of the rent has incurred an adjustment will be made to prepaid expenses.

Depreciation Expense

The second adjustment entry will be depreciation expense. This is the allocation of the cost of an asset as it is used over a period of time. Say you bought a new computer for your company. You will take the market value of that computer and figure out the lifespan of the computer. From there you can calculate the depreciation of the computer and make that adjustment under this expense.

One of the most common and even the easiest depreciation methods is the straight-line method. This is a system for calculating annual depreciation by subtracting an asset's salvage value from its cost and then dividing by its lifespan. This method is calculated based off every full year of use.

- Depreciation = (Cost – Salvage value) / Lifespan

Unearned Revenue

The third adjustment entry is called unearned revenue. This can also be called deferred revenue because the payment has been received for services that have not been provided. Unearned revenue is considered a liability. The adjustment is usually made when the services are provided. This can be monthly, quarterly, or annually.

Accrued Expense

The fourth type is accrued expense. This is when the cost is incurred during one month, quarter, or annual period but yet it is paid for in the next period.

Accrued Revenue

Finally, the last adjustment type is accrued revenue. This is much like the accrued expense. It is when the revenue is earned during one month, quarter, or annual period but yet the revenue is received in the next period. This adjustment will affect both revenue and assets. When revenue is accrued it creates the asset of a receivable.

Each of these adjustments must be figured into the company's trial balance. With that information you will prepare an adjusted trial balance. This will show a list of all accounts after all needed adjustments have been made so that it will reflect the revenues and expenses that were incurred for a specific date.

Chapter 7 – Completing the Accounting Cycle

As you go through the accounting cycle it is important to prepare and frequently update a company's journal, ledger, trial balance, and adjusted trial balance. As long as these statements and reports are updated then the company can get a clear picture of where the company is at that moment and help allow you to make decisions to move forward. These reports are generally done at the end of each month, quarterly, or in the annual accounting period. However, they could be done at any time to meet the needs of the company.

At the end of the annual accounting cycle, closing entries are made to reset and prepare the books for the next accounting period. The closing entries are the income summary, revenue, expenses, gains, losses, and owner's withdrawals or dividends.

The Worksheet

To help with the closing entries you can pull all your information from the journal, ledger, trial balance, and adjustment trial balance and put it into a worksheet. It is easy to make your closing entries when you have all your information consolidated into one worksheet. However, you may think it is too much work to consolidate the information. It is not necessary. The worksheet is simply a tool to help with resetting and preparing your closing entries.

The worksheet is divided into four sets of debits and credits. On the left side is a list of your accounts from the chart of accounts. Next will be the debits and credits for the trial balance, adjusting entries, income statement, and balance sheet from left to right. At the bottom of the columns will be the totals. The total debits should equal the total credits.

The total for the income statement columns represents net income. The balance sheet's debit column represents assets. The equivalent of its credits show liabilities plus owner's equity.

After all the transactions are posted to the ledger and a trial balance is prepared then you can start preparing the worksheet.

Start with listing each account in the left column of the worksheet. You will find this information in the chart of accounts.

Next, see the general ledger to find the trial balance figures of each account. Transfer this information to the debit and credit columns right after the account names. The balance will summarize all of the transactions for the time period before the adjusting entries are made. Remember if the account has a debit normal balance or a credit normal balance.

Next, find the adjusted amounts and enter them in the debit and credit columns to the right of the trial balance columns. Each adjustment should have a reference to the original adjustment in the ledger. This way if there were mistakes made in the adjustments you could find and fix them easily.

Next, take the adjusted amounts and enter them in the correct income statement and balance sheet columns. Always begin from the top and work your way down. Never skip around because you might forget one that needed to be recorded and will have your worksheet incorrect. Your revenue and expense accounts will be recorded in the income statement columns, while your assets, liabilities, and owner's equity accounts will be entered into the balance sheet columns.

Finally, total all the debits and credits at the bottom of the worksheet. Here you will look at the totals of the income statement columns to see the net income or loss for that time period. Check the balance sheet totals to find the assets, liabilities, and owner's equity.

Below is an example of the worksheet.

ABC Financial Company, Inc.

Worksheet

For the Month Ending July 31

ACCOUNT TITLE	Trial Balance		Adjustments		Income Statement		Balance Sheet	
	Debit	Credit	Debit	Credit	Debit	Credit	Debit	Credit

The worksheet is only a tool to help simplify preparing the closing statements. I would suggest that you take the time to create your own worksheet. This would save much time when it comes to close the book at the end of the cycle.

As you can see from the example worksheet, once you have all your totals transferred over to the worksheet it will allow you to easily find the information you are looking for.

If you are doing the books manually instead of using software such as QuickBooks, I would suggest creating a spreadsheet in Excel that will have your journal, ledgers, and worksheet in one file to automatically calculate the totals. This way you would have it done for you as you go.

Closing Entries

Finally, the last step of the accounting cycle is the closing entries. These are journal entries made to transfer a balance in revenue or expenses to the income summary on the income statement and the dividends account on the retained earnings statement. This is necessary to get ready for the new accounting cycle.

First, we need to create a temporary account called income summary. This is important as many of the closing entries affect this account in order to zero out those accounts.

The accounts that are closed at the end of the cycle are temporary accounts. Examples of these accounts are revenue, expenses, and dividends. These temporary accounts will never appear on the balance sheet. This is because the balance sheet only contains assets, liabilities, and owner's equity.

Most temporary accounts will be found on the income statement, except for dividends, they will appear on the statement of retained earnings.

You will also have permanent accounts such as assets, liabilities, and owner's equity. This will not be closed out at the end of the account cycle.

Types of Closing Entries

In order to prepare the books for the next cycle there are some accounts that need to be closed out. You must make these closing entries in the general ledger. They are:

1. Income summary—this is a temporary account that is created when you make the closing entries. All revenue and expense account balances will be transferred here. This will close those accounts and give then a zero balance. Once all entries are transferred to this account, the totals of the income summary will equal the company's net income or net loss for the year. Then the income statement will be closed out and transferred to the retained earnings statement.

2. Revenues—has a credit normal balance. Therefore, to close it out you need to debit revenue. Then it will be credited to the income statement.

3. Expenses—has a debit normal balance. Therefore to close it out you must credit the expense accounts. This will zero out expenses and you need to debit the income summary.

4. Dividends—these are the cash withdrawals that are given to shareholders for personal use. Keep in mind this account has a debit normal account. So we need to credit dividends so that it would have a zero balance. From there we will debit retained earnings. This is the only one that is not debited to the income summary and will go straight to the retained earnings.

Once the closing entries have been made and you have the income summary totals then you can calculate the net income or net loss on the income summary. You can then close the income summary to the retained earnings.

Once the books are closed then all the temporary accounts will have a zero balance and will be ready for the next accounting cycle. All the permanent accounts will carry over to the next accounting cycle.

Chapter 8 – Special Journals

Now that we have introduced you to the journals let's take a closer look at some of the special journals that you may come across.

Many times, a company will have repetitive transactions. For an example, your company may have a depreciation expense that must be applied every month. These companies may use a special journal for those transactions. Most of the time these special transactions are within the bigger companies that have many repetitive transactions.

These special journals are separate from the regular general journal. Mainly because it has transactions that are similar and occur often. For example, these journals may include sales journal, purchase journal, cash receipts journal, and cash disbursements journal. This is to only name a few.

Like the general journal, these special journals need to be posted to the ledgers. However, there are also subsidiary ledgers that they need to be posted to as well. These subsidiary ledgers have a control account in the general ledger that has a summary of the subsidiary ledger accounts which are more detailed. Subsidiary ledger accounts are where you will find a bulk of the company's detailed data.

Now you are probably asking yourself, "Wouldn't posting debits and credits to two different ledgers put the books off and not allow them to balance?" Actually, the general ledger is the main ledger that is used for all the books. The subsidiary ledger accounts are not part of the general ledger. All they are used for is to give more details about the accounts to support the numbers that are in the control account.

When you really think about it there are several good reasons for using a subsidiary ledger.

- They provide up-to-date information on specific account balances that is very detailed.

- They may also make it less likely to have errors by moving large amounts of numbers from the general ledger.
- When there are errors they may make it easier to find specific information, such as finding errors or tracking credit with customer and supplier accounts.
- They also make it possible to divide up the posting into more than one job. For example, you could have one employee post to the general ledger and another employee post to the subsidiary ledger. This will allow you to go through the books and see if the postings match. If they do not match it will give you an idea where to look for the errors.

Some of the common types of subsidiary ledgers are:
- Accounts Receivable Subsidiary Ledger
- Accounts Payable Subsidiary Ledger
- Some Fixed Assets Ledger
- Property, Plant, and Equipment (PPE)

Keep in mind that these subsidiary ledger accounts are based on the needs of the company. Let's take a look at some of these accounts.

Accounts Receivable

Anytime a customer buys a product and it is on credit you will record that transaction in accounts receivable. This is because there is no exchange of cash. This transaction will increase both revenue and assets. Since there is no exchange of cash at this time the cash account does not increase. Instead the accounts receivable is what increases. For example, your company delivered $400 of merchandise to a vendor and that vendor did not pay cash. Instead, the $400 was put on account as of December 2, 2015. To record this transaction, you would debit accounts receivable $400 due to it being bought on account. Even though it was bought on account it would still be considered as revenue. Therefore, you would credit the revenue account for $400. The transaction would like this:

Date	Account	Debit	Credit
December 2	Accounts receivable	$400	
	Revenue		$400

Now let's suppose the vendor pays the bill on account for $400 on January 3, 2016. You would then record that transaction on January 3 as a debit for $400 to cash. This is because you received cash for that account. You would then credit accounts receivable for the $400. This would be recorded like this:

Date	Account	Debit	Credit
January 3	Cash	$400	
	Accounts receivable		$400

So what would it look like if we did not pay on account? That would be recorded the same as the first transaction, except you would use cash instead of accounts receivable. Here you are buying on account and so you would need to create two separate transactions to move cash on account to cash in the bank. On the second transaction the revenue account is not affected because it had already been recorded on December 2, 2015. For this transaction we would record it in the subsidiary account like this:

	Debit	Credit
Beginning balance	$0	
December 2 delivery	$400	
January 3 payment		$400
Ending balance	$0	

Accounts Payable

Your company does not always only give credit to its customers or vendors. Sometimes credit is issued to the company. Anytime your company receives goods or services on credit then it is posted to the accounts payable. For example, you needed supplies for your company and you purchased these supplies on account. You made this transaction on December 2, 2015 for $400. You would then debit supplies for $400 as that is what you purchased on account and you have a supplies account in your chart of accounts. You would then credit accounts payable for $400 as you purchased supplies on account. Your transaction would look like this:

Date	Account	Debit	Credit
December 2	Supplies	$400	
	Accounts payable		$400

Now on January 3 you pay your account of $400 for your supplies. You will debit the accounts payable account for $400 as you are paying that amount off on the credit that was issued. Since you are paying cash for that credit you will credit cash for $400. Your transaction will look like this:

Date	Account	Debit	Credit
December 2	Accounts payable	$400	

	Cash		$400

Fixed Assets Ledger and the Property, Plant, and Equipment (PPE) Account

Your company may maintain a subsidiary ledger that is called fixed assets. However, a controlled ledger of the fixed assets ledger is known as the property, plant, and equipment, or PPE. Keep in mind that the accounts that are listed in the subsidiary account are dependent on the needs of your company. With this system all acquisitions of fixed asset debit will be listed under PPE.

To give you an idea of what accounts go to each subsidiary the following reference will help:

Accounts Receivable $1,000

- Al Forbush $300
- Jane Doe $200
- John Doe $500

Accounts Payable $1,000

- Toys Unlimited, Inc. $400
- Supplies Corp. $400
- Outsmart Clothing $200

PPE: Property, Plant, and Equipment $8,000

- Tables $2,000
- Car $3,000
- Computer $3,000

Sales Journal

The subsidiary ledgers can be posted from either the general or special journals. Every company has sales. Therefore, one of the most common special journals is the sales journal.

This journal will show all of the credit sales. Each entry will show in the sales journal and represent a debit to the customer's account in the accounts receivable. It will also show a credit to the revenue account. Keep in mind that cash receipts from those sales are recorded in a different special journal.

Cash Receipts Journal

Remember that in the sales journal the data has accounts on credit. These do not include cash sales. Those sales are recorded in the cash receipts journal. This special account includes three main parts for cash receipt.

1. Customers who have paid on account and are now paying cash on their account. The cash transaction is recorded here.
2. Any sales that were made and cash was paid.
3. Any other sources that the company took in cash.

Keep in mind that if there is a cash transaction, not on credit, then it will be recorded here. Also with this there are three debit columns that include:

1. Cash—which shows each transaction that involves a cash receipt.
2. Sales discounts—which if any discount was offered it will be recorded here.
3. Other—this includes any account that is different from sales discounts.

Much like the debits the credits also have three columns. They are:

1. Accounts Receivable—this is when a credit payment was included in the accounts receivable. Remember to write the name of that account in the details so that you know which account was paid.
2. Sales—this is where you will record all cash sales. It will match what was debited to cash.
3. Other—this is when a credit was to any fund that is incoming and is not from either of the other two columns.

Cash Receipts Joural page 21

Date	Account	Post ref.	Cash (Debit)	Sales (Debit)	Other (Debit)	Accounts receivable (Credit)	Sales (Credit)	Other (Credit)
7-Jan	Sales		$750				$750	
17-Jan	Richard Adams	Interest	$20					$20
27-Jan	Jean Webster		$488	$12		$500		
Total			$1,258	$12		$500	$750	$20

There are some entries that are posted in the cash receipts journal that are posted in both the subsidiary and general ledgers.

When posting these transactions, you would put a check in the post ref. as it has been consolidated. However, in the general journal you would put a code in this column such as CR21. This would refer to where it was posted. Such as Cash Receipt (CR) and page 21 (21) of the cash receipt. This would make it easier to see where cash is coming from. There are some transactions that are not posted in the cash receipts journal but are still posted in the subsidiary ledgers. For example, interest, rents, or dividends are posted directly to the general ledgers.

Purchases Journal

When you purchase inventory on credit you will record it in the purchases journal. These transactions are made based on the recourse such as a purchase invoice. This journal is mainly used for the purchases of inventory.

When you post in the purchases journal you would debit the purchases account and credit the accounts payable in the general ledger. This journal is used much like the sales journal. Every invoice in the purchases journal is on a single line.

The information you will have in the purchases journal are:

1. Date of transaction
2. Supplier's name
3. Invoice date
4. Amount

In some cases, there will be a fifth column that will list the terms.

See the following example of a purchase journal:

		Purchases Journal				Page 1
Date	Supplier	Invoice Date	Post ref.	Amount (debit purchases/credit accounts payable)	Terms
5-Jan	Silk Shop	5-Jan		$300	
15-Jan	Sunbrella, Inc	20-Jan		$700	
25-Jan	Cushion Boutique	31-Jan		$450	

Each day you would post the amounts in the account holder's name. You will check off the post ref. when you consolidate the journal and ledgers. However, in accounts payable ledger you will put a P1 in the post ref. This represents purchases Journal (P) and the page number (1).

Cash Disbursements Journal

Since all purchases on credit are recorded in the purchases journal, where are purchases recorded when cash is used? These transactions are recorded in the cash disbursements journal. Although, these are not always only purchases that are made with cash. They also include transactions when you pay cash on an account when you purchased with credit. The format is similar to that of the cash receipts journal.

Here you will have three columns for the credits. They are:

1. Cash
2. Purchase discounts
3. Other accounts

You will also have two columns for the debits. These include:

1. Accounts payable
2. Other accounts

The cash disbursements journal may look like this:

					Cash Disbursements Journal				page 3
Date	Check #	Payee	Account	Post ref.	Debits			Credits	
					Cash	Purchase discounts	Other accounts	Accounts payable	Other accounts
11-Feb	112	Triad Used Cars		J8	$75			$75	
13-Feb	113	Triad Tribune		J8	$125	$25		$150	
27-Feb	114	Triad Real Estate	Rent expense	J8	$2,000				$2,000
28-Feb	115	Petty cash	Petty cash expense	J8	$50				$50

The accounts that are posted in this journal are also posted to the accounts payable subsidiary ledger.

General Journal Transactions

Every transaction would be included in a journal. However, not all of the transactions will fit into a special journal. For instance, those transactions that are not involved with credit sales, cash receipts, purchases, or cash disbursements will be in the general journal and may be detailed enough from there.

Take for example transactions that include sales and purchase returns and allowances, notes payable, and notes receivable. These will be those types of transactions.

Although, just because the transactions are not always posted to the special journals they may still be posted to the subsidiary ledgers. The general journal is used to record all types of transactions. That means that it is a history of all the transactions that your company will have. Usually the transactions that are not posted and do not fit in the special journals are ones that are left over and are usually nonrecurring, dissimilar, or infrequent, for example, adjustments entries, closing entries, and correcting entries.

Chapter 9 – Accounts Receivables

Many companies have their own accounts receivable team. It is so important that I needed to add a chapter just for that.

Most companies would prefer to receive payments in cash. I know I would rather have a payment in cash than to have someone owing me money on credit. However, there are times that a company may choose to extend a line of credit. Now with extending a line of credit we start using an accounts receivable account. This way we would be able to keep track of these transactions.

A really good way of looking at this in our everyday lives is when you get a loan or a credit card. The bank extends you a line of credit and in return you pay for it at a later date. They may add interest to this payment so that you would get it paid quicker.

Accounts Receivable

How often have you bought something on account? The accounts receivable is just that. When a company makes a sale on credit and does not immediately receive a cash payment it is recorded as an account receivable.

Credit payments such as accounts receivable is a promise-to-pay-in-the-future type of account and will be considered an asset. This is because you extended a line of credit to a customer and they will pay you in cash at a future date.

There are times when a company will give terms as to when the payment is due, such as net 30. This means that payment is due in 30 days from the date on the invoice or receipt. There are other times when a company may offer a discount. This generally looks like this: 4/10 net 30. This means that if the client pays the amount due in 10 days they will receive a 4% discount. Otherwise it is due in 30 days in full.

When you're accounting for the receivable you will need to record the credit transaction in the sales journal. However, this is not the only transaction that needs to be made. You will also need to record it in the accounts receivable ledger and the customer's accounts receivable account.

Notes Receivable

We just got through talking about accounts receivable. So what is notes receivable? You would think they were the same. However, they are different. While accounts receivable is about a delay in payment, notes receivable is more like a loan. This is also known as an asset to the company. Normally with a notes receivable there will be interest that will be charged to the amount over time as outlined in the terms of the promissory note or contract for the note.

Notes receivable is one account that must comply with the GAAP standards in both the way it is recorded and the reports. When looking at the components that are involved you will look at the following:

- Maturity date
- Duration of note
- Interest and interest rate
- Maturity value

These are the main components.

Methods for Uncollectible Accounts

You will come across times when someone could not pay their bill or honor their contract that was signed. Now we need to attempt to collect it and if we cannot then we will need to use one of the methods for recording and handling that debt.

Let's first look at the direct write-off method. This is a system for dealing with the uncollectible accounts. With this method a company will remove the entire account from the books as soon as it is recognized as being uncollectible. However, many times a bill may be paid after it is considered uncollectible. When this happens, you would do a reversal entry. Basically, this is just that. You add the account back on the books and make the transaction of it being paid.

There is also the allowance method. Much like the direct write-off method the allowance method is about recognizing the uncollectible account. However, with this method it is based on matching principle. When using the accrual accounting, all the expenses must be matched with the related revenue. This would be done within the same accounting period. Once these are matched then the estimated amount that is recorded and is expected to be written off for the bad debit would be considered the allowance for uncollectible accounts.

We also have the percent of net credit sales method. This is also known as net sales method. For this method we need to consider how much net sales the company will not be collecting. For use to calculate this figure we need to look at prior years' uncollectible debits. Ask yourself, how much has your company written off as a percentage of credit sales for those years? Once you have that answer then you will use that information to get an estimate of the percentage of credit sales for the current year. Here is the formula for figuring out the answer to how much will be given in this method:

- % of uncollectible bad debt * % total credit sales = ????

There also is the percent of receivables method which uses percentages of the amounts in the accounts receivable ledger. These percentages give an estimate on how much money is owed to your company but will not be collectible.

The aging of accounts receivable method is similar, although this method estimates the uncollectible accounts in more detail. The accounts would be grouped into categories based on how much time has passed since the date of the sale. Keep in mind the longer the account is outstanding, the more likely it will not be collected.

There will be times that a client will pay money towards an account that had been written off as bad credit. This would require two transactions.

1. The reversal—it is that simple. We need to reverse the write-off. Easy way to remember this is that we need to put the account back on the books so that we can accept the payment.
2. Cash transaction—we need to record the money coming in for this account.

Let's take a look at these two transactions. The first one is to reverse the write-off.

DATE	ACCOUNT	DEBIT	CREDIT
May 15	Accounts receivable, Al's Construction	$500	
	Allowance for uncollectible accounts		$500

Now that we reversed the write-off and put the account back on the books we need to accept the payment from Al's Construction.

DATE	ACCOUNT	DEBIT	CREDIT
May 15	Cash	$500	
	Accounts receivable, Al's Construction		$500

Financial Statement Presentation

So far, we have gone over a great deal of information in accounting. Even with bad credit it needs to be reported on the financial statements. So when you look at the accounts receivable and bad debit you would only get a small part of the company's financial condition. To really understand your financial conditions, you would need to look at all the financial statements.

There are typically four financial statements that an accountant will prepare. They are:

1. The income statement
2. The statement of owner's equity
3. The balance sheet
4. The statement of cash flows

These statements will give a good understanding of how well the company is doing for a particular accounting period or a specific point in time such as at the end of a given month.

It is important that these financial statements are accurate. Investors rely on this information so that they can make good decisions about their investments.

Maturity Date

The maturity date is when the note needs to be paid. The terms of the note can tell you when the maturity date will be in a few ways. Sometimes it will be listed as a specific date. It can also be listed as a specific month. Finally, it could also be listed as a number of days after the date the note was signed.

When you look at the number of days between the date the note was signed and the maturity date it is known as the duration of the note. Another thing to look at is the interest that is incurred. This can be calculated based on the duration or number of days of the note and the interest. It is based on a daily rate. However, there are times you can base it on a monthly or yearly rate if it is outlined in the note.

When a note is signed it will outline the terms of the contract; that is, to include the interest rate. Just like any loan this is a fixed percentage of the amount that was borrowed.

To find out what the interest will be you can use this formula:

- Interest = Principle * Rate * Time

Let's also look at each area so that you will know where to find the principle, rate, and time.

- Principle—the amount of money borrowed. This is the original amount with no added interest or fees.
- Rate—interest rate expressed as a decimal, found in the terms of the contract.

- Time—the duration of the note divided by 360.

For example, you have a note for 90 days. It was written for $3,000 with an 8% rate. The equation would look like this:

- Interest = $3,000 * 0.08 * (90/360)
- Interest = $3,000 * 0.08 * 0.25
- $60 = $3,000 * 008 * 0.25

Now that you know the interest you can find the maturity value. To do this simply add the worth of the note and the interest. So for this example the maturity value would be $3,060.

Interest Income

Whenever a company issues a promissory note, whether it is to buyers for goods and services or you are dealing with investments in stocks and securities, you must account for the interest income. This will be earned on these assets.

Anytime you earn interest on these notes or contracts then the interest income account will increase. This interest must be reported as revenue on the income statement.

Many companies are not lenders. However, they may need to borrow money for their company. This would be recorded as an interest expense as you would be paying interest on the notes that you borrowed on.

When recording interest and keeping track of it you would need to make two transactions to record these. The first one will be a debit to cash and a credit to notes payable.

DATE	ACCOUNT	DEBIT	CREDIT
April 1	Cash	$2,000	
	Notes payable		$2,000

The second transaction will be a debit to notes payable of the principle amount, a debit to interest expense to show that amount of interest, and a credit to the cash account that combines the two amounts.

DATE	ACCOUNT	DEBIT	CREDIT
May 31	Notes payable	$2,000	
	Interest expense	$17	
	Cash		$2,017

No matter if you are tracking the interest or other payments, the accounts receivables will help a company track all the money coming into the company. This will give you a good idea as to where the company is heading.

Chapter 10 – Liabilities and Payroll

All companies will have some sort of liability and most will have employees and need to figure in the payroll for their staff. The current liabilities are separated into two categories or sections: known liabilities and estimated liabilities.

Known Liabilities

Any time a company has obligations that carry a set value you have a known liability. The known liabilities may fall into other categories such as:

- Accounts payable
- Sales tax payable
- Unearned revenue
- Short-term notes payable
- Payroll liabilities
- Accrued liabilities

If you remember, any goods or services purchased on credit are considered accounts payable. However, when you make a sale it may incur yet another type of known liability. This would be sales tax payable. This account will be used for tracking and recording sales tax that needs to be paid to the state and local governments.

Also remember when a company receives money in advance it would be considered as unearned revenue. These unearned incomes can be considered as a known liability.

Another form of known liability is a short-term note payable. This is a debt that will be paid on a promissory note within one year.

An important known liability for a business is the payroll liability. The best way to think about these liabilities is the amount paid to employees and is a set amount paid on a predetermined date. This type of liability has three categories.

- Employee compensation
- Payroll withholdings
- Payroll taxes

For this we can look at your regular paycheck. You perform 40 hours a week for two weeks at $9 per hour. This earns you $720. This would be considered your employee compensation. From that $750 there are withholdings that are deducted to fulfill tax requirements. These payroll withholdings are social security, Medicare, and federal and state income taxes. However, social security and Medicare taxes support benefits such as retirees, disabled individuals, and other types of medical programs. Instead of employees needing to pay their federal and state taxes directly to the government, your business is required to deduct this and report it for the employee. The last one is the payroll taxes. There are the withholdings from the employees that need to be paid to the government. For an idea of how this is paid see the example:

DATE	ACCOUNT	DEBIT	CREDIT
July 31	Salary wage expense	$1,330	
	Social security tax payable		$200
	Medicare tax payable		$30
	Federal income tax payable		$1,100

There are times where an employee may request to have additional withholdings deducted from their wages. The most common are:

- Insurance premium payments
- Pension or retirement plan

These are known liabilities because they are set amounts of payment established in advance.

Estimated Liabilities

Obligations with a set value are known as liabilities. So what are estimated liabilities? So far we have talked a lot about accounts that hold a set value. Many companies also have obligations that are not a set amount. These amounts will be determined at a future date. Therefore, we need to estimate what the value will be. Some of the accounts that will listed as estimated liabilities are:

- Employee benefits
- Income taxes

- Warranties
- Lawsuits

Employee Benefits

Things like vacation pay and bonuses will be considered as employee benefits. These types of benefits are considered as estimated liabilities because they are promised to be paid at a later date.

Let's take for instance vacation pay. For each hour or day an employee works they earn vacation time that they can take at a later time. When the employee takes the time off then the business considers this as a liability. Vacation time is only an estimated liability because out of that time earned, the employer does not know how much time the employee will take off. For this time of entry you would debit vacation pay expense and credit the wages payable account to accommodate for the vacation time that was taken.

DATE	ACCOUNT	DEBIT	CREDIT
June 30	Vacation pay expense	$125	
	Wages payable		$125

Many times, bonuses may be offered for performance are other types of tasks. These bonuses can also be considered a liability and are only estimated as the employer does not know how much of a bonus will be earned by the employee. Bonuses are handled in a similar manner to that of vacation pay. You would debit bonus expense and credit wages payable.

DATE	ACCOUNT	DEBIT	CREDIT
December 31	Bonus expense	$5,000	
	Wages payable		$5,000

Contingent Liabilities

When I first looked at contingent liabilities my first thought was, what is that? Then as I did some research I realized that anytime a business faces the threat of a potential liability that may or may not occur in the future, it would be considered a contingent liability. These are only accrued when they are likely to occur. Many of these types of liabilities that are not accrued must be disclosed in notes to the financial statements. A good example of this type of liability is a product warranty.

Take Al's Ladders, Inc., for example. They had a gross sales in the month of June. The business estimated that 5% of its sales, or $2,500, would be allocated for product warranty liability.

DATE	ACCOUNT	DEBIT	CREDIT
June 30	Cash	$50,000	

	Sales		$50,000
June 30	Warranty expense	$2,500	
	Warranty liability		$2,500

Then by July 7, the business had accrual figure for the warranty liability of $3,000 in repairs for ladders covered by the warranty. If you notice, in this example the accrued amount is over the $2,500 that was set aside for the liability. It went over by $500. So now what do we need to do?

DATE	ACCOUNT	DEBIT	CREDIT
July 7	Warranty expense	$500	
	Warranty liability	$2,500	
	Cash		$3,000

Depending on how likely an occurrence is, a contingent liability can be classified into three types.

1. Probable
2. Reasonable
3. Remote

The type of contingent liability that is most likely to occur and has a cost that is reasonably estimated is a probable liability. This would be shown as a debit to warranty expense and a credit to warranty liability on the balance sheet.

Occasionally you will get a contingent liability that could possibly occur but is less likely to happen than a probable liability. These are known as reasonably possible liabilities. This will be recorded as a footnote in the financial statements with no further action required.

The last contingent liability is the remote liability. These are the least likely to occur. These do not need to be listed or recorded.

Chapter 11 – Current and Long-term Assets

Now that we have gone over some of the liabilities that may occur in a business, it is time to look at the assets. The first thing we will look at are the current assets. These are highly important to a business as they allow accountants and investors to learn more about them.

To give you an idea of how this is achieved, an investor will divide the total assets by the current liabilities to calculate the business current ratio.

- Current Ratio = total current assets / current liabilities

If the business has a higher ratio then it will determine that it has a high liquidity. However, if the ratio is less than 1, then the business may not have enough liquidity to cover the short-term expenses.

The current assets have several different categories. The main three kinds of current assets are:

- Cash
- Short-term investments
- Trade accounts receivable

Cash

As you know, cash refers to money. This money can be in the form of currency or equivalent to currency. Cash, unlike investments, can be accessed easily and quickly. This can be used to cover short-term debts and daily business expenses. Now because cash is such a vital part of the daily operations it also has a vital part in the internal controls.

It is important to ensure that cash is reported accurately. Investors use this information to make important decisions. With that said you should always have your balance sheet up to date and accurate at all times. It should be free of errors and a reliable source. Therefore, to ensure accurate information is presented it will show and distinguish assets, liabilities, and equity. To take it a step further, assets should be split into three areas such as current assets, fixed assets, and other assets.

1. Assets
- Current assets—include cash and cash equivalent, accounts receivable, and inventory.
- Fixed assets—include property, land, buildings, and machinery.
- Other assets—include anything not covered in the other two.
2. Liabilities
3. Equity

Short-Term Investments

The second of the main types are short-term investments. These are just that, short term, which means that they mature within 12 months, whereas cash equivalents mature within 90 days.

To ensure that the asset reporting is accurate then it needs all the valid and necessary disclosures. A disclosure that is regarding any transfer of assets that have occurred within a year or reporting period needs to be made in the notes of the financial statements. If a liability is no longer on the books or a new asset has been added then it needs to be classified and reported in the notes of the balance sheet.

These short-term investments are products that a business intends to change into cash. When you think about short term it will always be less than one year. Most of the time these investments are low risk. Therefore, the returns are also low.

The two main types of short-term investments are debt securities and equity securities.

Debt securities are also known as a debt instrument or a fixed-income security. They are a portion of an organization's debt that can be bought or sold. With that being said, when an investor buys a debt security then they are buying a part of the business's debt. These securities have clearly defined terms. The terms are typically identified in a contract so that the investor fully understands them.

The other kind of security are equity securities. These represent ownership in a corporation. These investors will also have a say as to the fate of the corporation. With that they will also be affected by any gains or losses that corporation may have. Another name for these is stocks of a corporation. However, corporations are not the only businesses that can issue stocks. A non-corporation such as a sole proprietorship or a partnership do not sale stock; however, they can issue stock shares to employees giving them partial ownership of the business.

Let's say you are an investor and would like to know what your percentage of ownership is for the company.

- % of ownership = number of shares / total number of outstanding shares

Outstanding shares are the total number of shares sold by the company.

Trade Accounts Receivable

Trade accounts receivable will directly be related to product sales and services provided. Think about it. When an item is sold on credit, there will be some customers that will pay sooner than others, and some will never pay.

The real question is, how many accounts receivable can you hold? What happens if you hold too many or not enough?

Let's take a look at what an investor may think if you have too few accounts receivable. They may think that your credit extension is too restrictive, limiting potential sales. It could also say that maybe the policies are poised to write-off bad debt too fast when you could still have a chance to collect it.

Although, keep in mind that having too many accounts receivable may create different problems. Having too many may put the business at risk and lower liquidity of the company. It may show an investor that a company will have a hard time covering outstanding expenses. This will also give a risk to some customers not being creditworthy and they may default their accounts.

As we discussed earlier, businesses that extend credit may have issues with uncollectible accounts. There are times that with these accounts you can extend a discount so that they can pay off the account.

Long-Term Assets

Besides just the current assets there are some long-term assets. These assets are usually assets that you hold for periods that are more than one year. These also represent the future growth of the business.

Some of these long-term assets can include but are not limited to:

- Land

- Vehicles
- Computers
- Machinery
- Equipment
- Securities
    - Stocks
    - Bonds

Businesses use these long-term assets to produce revenue. The longer the asset the better. It will cut costs and make the business produce more income. This will also make your business more valuable. In return it will increase stock prices. However, you do need to be careful. It is possible to have too many long-term assets. If you have too many then the company or business may not have enough capital and could have trouble keeping up with expenses and liabilities. However, on another note, having too few long-term assets could also harm the company. This could make it vulnerable to changes and difficult to fight against the competitors.

Fixed Assets

With fixed assets the main purpose is to create revenue. These types of assets are not to be sold. Even though fixed assets cannot be turned into cash they do enhance the value of your company.

Due to the GAAP a fixed asset must be recorded on a balance sheet at a cost value and not market value. This is considered a historical cost principle. There are several reasons why they are treated as a historical cost principle.

1. Cost can be easily verified in an audit. This is done by checking a receipt. Whereas, market value is highly subjective.

2. When a company starts it is assumed that they are not going to be selling off assets and shutting down. As long as the business intends to stay in business the market value of a fixed asset is irrelevant. This is because the function of the asset is to produce revenue and not to be sold.

3. According to the GAAP it is required for a company to recognize revenue and expenses in a financial period when they are earned or incurred.

4. The initial cost of an asset was recorded on the balance sheet when it was purchased. Therefore, the amount of depreciation must be listed as an expense over the span of life used for that asset.

Land is one of the most common and expensive fixed assets. It will include everything on ground (for example grass, fences, and trees), over the ground (for example air, space), and under the ground (such as minerals). It is supposed to have the longest lifespan or even indefinite. This is because the only thing that may shorten the lifespan of land is a natural disaster. This is a valuable asset as it usually is not used up, destroyed, or stolen. On the balance sheet it will reflect the cost of the land. With that it will also include incidental cost such as surveys, insurance, legal fees, and property taxes.

Buildings, much like land, are expensive and a valuable fixed asset. They indirectly produce revenue. The cost of acquiring buildings usually includes insurance, closing costs, taxes, and the purchase price. They do not last forever. Therefore, they have a finite lifespan.

For all business your equipment is essential. Much like buildings they indirectly produce revenue. The cost of equipment generally includes the purchase price, sales tax, and delivery fees.

While looking at the long-term assets you need to remember that any asset that is purchased and lasts more than one year is a capital expenditure. These expenditures are recorded on the balance sheet. Usually they include large purchases that bring a lot of value to your company or business. These will not be listed in expenses because they will not be used up in the current accounting period.

So we talked about the bigger assets but what about the smaller ones such as a coffee maker, trashcan, or a light bulb? These are considered revenue expenditures. These will last several accounting periods. Even though $500 is a common limit for the maximum cost of this type of expenditure it can vary based on the company or business. These assets are not recorded in the balance sheet. They are usually listed as an expense to make it easy to record them.

Depreciation

With long-term assets you will have many assets that will depreciate over time. Land is the one thing that is the exception to depreciation. Mainly because land does not depreciate. Depreciation is for those assets that are good for only a given number of years and will eventually need to be replaced. Therefore, we need to figure out how much it will depreciate over time.

Depreciation will assign a cost of a long-term asset to an expense account in the periods when the asset generates revenue. So when you think about it, depreciation basically offsets the revenue of an accounting period with the costs of the product or service consumed to generate the revenue.

The depreciation expense does not come to decrease value. Instead it is a result from allocating cost of a period of time. Once you start using the asset that is to be depreciated it is generally done quarterly or annually. The depreciation ends when the company or businesses disposes of the asset or determines that its lifespan is over.

There are several ways to record depreciation. The GAAP rule only requires the method used is rational and systematic through the asset's lifespan. Let's look at some of the ways to figure and record depreciation.

Straight-line method—this is the most common for financial reporting. It will maximize net income more than any other method. It is also the easiest to understand and follow the calculations. This method attributes an equal amount of expense to each period of lifespan for the assets. Before we can understand the calculations we first need to find out what salvage value is. When a business uses the lifespan of the asset and is ready to sale it you need to ask yourself how much you expect to earn from selling the asset. This is the salvage value. So let's look at the equation for the straight-line method:

- Depreciation = (Cost – Salvage Value) / Lifespan

To explain this better let's look at each aspect of the equation. First you will take the cost of the asset and subtract the salvage value. The cost will be the original cost when you purchased the asset. Then you will take this total and divide it by the lifespan. The lifespan is the number of years that the business sees the asset as useful. This gives you the depreciation cost.

For example, you have a flow jet for your business. The estimated lifespan is five years. You originally purchased it for $20,000 and the estimated salvage value would be $5,000. Let's put this in the equation. $20,000 - $5,000 = $15,000 / 5 = $3,000. Therefore, the depreciation will be $3,000. Many times, you can think of the lifespan as a percentage. The rate is 1. So the lifespan for the flow jet will be 1/5 or 20%.

With a depreciation schedule we see the book value. It is important to know the book value of an asset. To find this you will take the original asset cost and minus the accumulated depreciation.

- Book Value = Cost – Accumulated Depreciation

Market value and book value are not the same. Book value represents the value of the asset according to the business books. Each year the book value has to be updated. This is because the accumulated depreciation will change each year and the company or business needs to know when the lifespan will be up. However, the book value should never go below the salvage value of the asset. This is a conservation principle. Keep in mind that when the depreciation is finished you will see the salvage value and the book value will be equal.

Declining-balance method—with this method the depreciation assigned for each year of usage is different. Suppose that you feel that your asset is more productive and creates more revenue early in its life. This method is an accelerated method. You will see more depreciation expense allocated early in the asset's life than it would be in the later years. For the declining-balance method we can calculate the depreciation expense with the following formula:

- Depreciation Expense = Rate * Current Book Value

Since the book value decreases each period so does the depreciation expense. This is why it is called declining-balance method.

With all the methods you need to keep in mind that the book value will never go below its salvage value and it will be equal when it is at the end of its lifespan.

Sum of the Years' Digits (SOYD) method—is another accelerated method for depreciation. With this method the amount of depreciation is assigned to each year of life based on an inverted scale of the sum of the years of its lifespan.

Units of Production method—is different than the other methods. It is based on depreciation from a measurement of the asset's output instead of its lifespan. With this method it allows for more depreciation when the asset is used more. The method is more used for assets such as vehicles and machinery. For calculating this method you would use the following formula. It is similar to the formula for the straight-line method.

- Depreciation Rate per Unit = (Cost – Salvage Value) / Estimated Units of Output

Keep in mind that natural resources are depreciated differently than other assets. This is because once their lifespan is up or they are used up then they can only be replaced through natural processes. To figure this you will need to first find the cost per unit.

- Cost Per Unit = Depletable Cost / Estimated Total Number of Units

Once you have the cost per unit then you can calculate the depletion expense.

- Depletion Expense = Cost Per Unit * Yearly Number of Units Extracted

Modified Accelerated Cost of Recovery System (MACRS) method—must be used for a business's income tax returns. Businesses are allowed to use one method for their income tax returns and another method for their financial statements. With this method the Internal Revenue Service (IRS) will specify depreciation rates and time periods for particular categories of fixed assets, for example, furniture and computer equipment. Using this method will lower net income which will lower the taxes owed to the IRS.

Chapter 12 – Owner's Equity

With the accounting equation we have taken a closer look at the assets and liabilities. Now let's take a look at the owner's equity. This can also be considered as stockholder's equity. As we have learned if you take the liabilities and subtract them from assets you get the owner's equity. Therefore, this is what is left over for the company's owners. This also includes contributions of capital by the owners. These contributions are used to fund the operations of the company as well as any undistributed net income or net loss. Here is where you will see the worth of your company.

Suppose you purchase a car for 40,000 on which you put a down payment of 20%. This would leave 80% to the bank. Therefore, you will have 20% or $8,000 of equity. As you make payments your equity will go up until you fully pay it off and have 100% equity of the car.

There are primarily two types of owner's equity.

1. Contributed capital—for sole proprietor or partnership in cash or assets, for example, land, buildings, or equipment. They value a fair market value. With corporations the capital generally comes from proceeds of stock sales.

2. Earner capital—is the cumulative value of net income or net loss that is not taken out of the business. These funds are left to generate future income and growth.

Some Differences Between Sole Proprietorship and Corporation Equity

With a sole proprietorship there are three primary owner's equity accounts.

1. Contributed capital—money that is contributed by the individual or partnership to the company.

2. Undistributed income—earnings that the owner leaves in the business to fund future growth.
3. Owner's drawing—cash that is withdrawn from the business for personal use.

Corporations are mainly funded from stock sales and earnings retained from the company. The following chart will help you better understand what types of owner's equity are used for the type of company.

ACCOUNT NAME	SOLE PROPRIETORSHIP	PARTNERSHIP	CORPORATION
Owner's Equity	Yes	Yes	
Owner's Drawing	Yes	Yes	
Undistributed Income	Yes	Yes	
Common Stock			Yes
Preferred Stock			Yes
Treasury Stock			Yes
Additional Paid-In Capital			Yes
Retained Earnings			Yes

Recording for Different Company Types

Sole Proprietorship—is not a corporation. It is owned by one person. That individual holds the future of the business in their hands. They will make all the decisions, take all the risks, and enjoy all the gains of the business. The main advantage for this type of business is how simple it is. However, like everything when you have advantages there are just as many disadvantages. One of the main disadvantages is the owner's unlimited liability; that is, you are responsible for all the actions of the business, both good and bad. Which means this will put all the assets at risk. Not just the business assets but your personal assets too. Sole proprietorships and partnerships are handled much the same way.

Corporations—are legal entities that are separate from their owners. A corporation, so to speak, has a life of its own. They exist until legally dissolved. The owners are not one individual or even a group of people that form a partnership in the business. The owners of a corporation are its shareholders or stockholders. However, they are not personally responsible for the debt of the company. Because of this limited liability structure, it makes a corporation desirable for most of the large and medium businesses to include many of the smaller ones.

The publicly held corporations need to follow regulations and reporting requirements from various authorities such as:

- Securities and Exchange Commission (SEC)
- Secretary of State
- Internal Revenue Service (IRS)
- State and local taxing authorities

This is only a few and the major authorities that are involved. They may be subject to many others as well.

For a corporation they are required to submit financial statements that include the following:

1. Income statement
2. Balance sheet
3. Statement of cash flows
4. Retained earnings statements

The following chart will outline how each source outlines its responsibilities in a corporation.

SOURCE	RESPONSIBILITIES
Secretary of State	Approves the articles of incorporation, which state the number and classes of authorized shares and the associated par value, if any, and any amendments to the articles.
Board of Directors	Authorizes issues and repurchasing of shares including the dollar value allocated for repurchases. Authorizes the payment of dividends, and specifies the amount, date of record, and date of payment.
Shareholders	Approves authorizing additional shares, generally at the annual meeting. Approves election of members of the board of directors; nonbinding vote on executive compensation.
Controller	Records in the corporate ledger the proceeds from sale and repurchase of shares of stock.
Corporate Treasurer	Keeps any hard copy stock certificates in a secure, locked

or Secretary	location.
	Retains minutes of board meetings.
Third-Party Securities Dealers	Sells the stock in the market, collects proceeds of the sale, and remits them to the company.

Since a corporation relies on stocks and retained earnings then the equity is different than that of a sole proprietorship or a partnership. Before the shares are issued for a corporation they need to first be authorized by the board of directors and then approved by the state's secretary of state during the time the corporation files their incorporation registration. Let's look at some of the equities that a corporation may have.

- Common Stock—is known as the voting stock for the corporation. For each share you will get one vote at the company's annual meeting. Say you have 20 stocks. That would give you 20 votes at the meeting. They also elect the board of directors, approve the selection of the audit firm that will audit the financials, and approve executive compensation plans and the frequency of approving executive compensation.

- Preferred Stock—is a nonvoting stock. Because it does not have voting rates it generally has a fixed dividend rate. This way it will pay out a greater dividend in exchange of the voting privileges.

- Treasury Stock—comes from when a company repurchases a stock share that was previously issued instead of retiring it.

- Par Value—is the book value that is assigned to the stock and the minimum price the share is originally offered for sale. Not all companies have a par value assigned to their stocks.

- Additional Paid-In Capital—is simply the difference between the stock selling price and the par value.

Partnerships

With a partnership you share the responsibilities of the business. You can have a general partner that has unlimited liability of the company but you may have a limited liability partner that is only limited to what is decided in the partnership. A partnership is much like a sole proprietorship.

The flowing chart will help you see a better picture of the characteristics of the three types of businesses.

CHARACTERISTIC	SOLE PROPRIETORSHIP	PARTNERSHIP	CORPORATION
Number of Owners	One	Two or more	Based on number of shares

Ease of setup	No legal agreement	Legal agreement needed	Articles of incorporation, authorization of shares of stock, etc.
Owner's Liability	Unlimited	At least one partner is unlimited; others may be limited	Limited
Life	Life of the owner	Limited life based on partners	Perpetual life
Net Income	Belongs to proprietor	Passed through to the partners	Distributed as dividends
Tax Reporting	Owner's tax returns—1040 Schedule C for business income	Partnership information return and partner's individual returns; income is taxed when earned	Corporate tax return; individual shareholders must report and pay taxes on dividends; corporation is taxed when profit is earned, but shareholders are taxed only when they receive dividends or sell stock.
Regulatory fillings	Depends on the industry	Depends on the industry	SEC for publicly owned companies regardless of industry.
Means of raising capital	Owner contribution	Partners' contribution	Sale of stock

Chapter 13 – Income Statement

We mentioned earlier about the financial statements that are needed to be completed so that we can have a good outlook of where your business is. One of those statements is the income statement. We are going to take a closer look at the income statements and what is involved in them.

These statements are essential to the business as they will show profits and losses. They will also give the management and stockholders information for making good business decisions, borrowing money, and growing your business with products and services.

The income statement is also known as the statement of operations, the statement of income, and the profit-and-loss statement. One thing to remember is the matching principle. This term is referred to in accounting practices when you pair revenue with the cost, or expense that was incurred to generate that revenue.

Revenue

If you remember, a business's revenue refers to the sum of money earned. This money can come from products sold or services rendered for a certain period of time. This is also known as the gross earnings. These are sales revenue before you subtract any discounts or sale returns that are generated from a specific business activity. Any revenues will increase owner's equity and are usually recorded quarterly. Keep in mind that the transactions that usually generate revenue are:

- Selling goods
- Selling assets
- Providing services
- Leasing or renting business assets

Sales and Revenue

On an income statement generally, sales and revenue are treated as the same thing. This is because they both increase equity. Although there is one main difference. Sales or the revenue from sales is generated from normal business operations, while other revenue may be generated from activities that are not normal business operations. Some income statements label revenue as sales or sales revenue.

Now we have sales revenue, which is labeled as sales revenue on the income statement. What about revenue that is not from sales? This revenue is labeled as other revenue and would be included in a different part of the income statement.

Revenue is recognized and recorded as sales as soon as each sale has taken place. This is to include when credit is used instead of cash being received right away. The revenue will still be recognized at the time of sale and not when payment for the credit is received. I need you to remember, as it is important, that when revenue is being recognized in the accrual-based accounting it requires the expenses to match with revenue during a given accounting period.

Expenses

Just like revenue, expenses also need to be recognized and recorded at the right time. Keep in mind that expenses are recognized and recorded at the time they occur. Even if the expense has not been paid yet and is only billed or invoiced they are recorded at the time of billing or invoicing. Expenses occur in order to generate revenue. There is a saying, "You need to spend money to make money." That statement is very true. Anytime you start a business you will need to spend money for land, business equipment, buildings, and supplies. All these items take money. However, all these items generate revenue in their own way. Because of this the expenses must appear on the income statement during the time it relates to the sales revenue.

For either merchandise or manufacturing types of companies you will have cost of goods sold. For merchandisers, the cost of goods sold will refer to the cost of inventory that is acquired for resale. Two good examples for this are Amazon and Walmart. They do not make their own products. Instead, they buy its inventory from other companies and then resell them to the consumers. When the product is purchased for resell and added to the inventory it is recorded as an expense on the income statement during the time the product was purchased.

Operating Expenses

Operating expenses are also recorded on the income statement after revenues. These are expenses that occur that come from running a business. These could include:

- Salaries paid
- Research and development

- Legal fees
- Bank charges
- Accounting fees
- Rent
- Lease payments
- Utility bills
- Fee for business licenses

Keep in mind that if an expense does not fall under cost of goods sold then it should fall under operating expenses on the income statement. Note that if it is fixed or variable operating expenses they need to be recorded separately on the income statement.

There are three main categories of operating expenses.

1. Selling expenses—are directly related to making sales or generating revenue, for example, wages, advertising, travel, entertainment, rent, utilities, telephone, commissions, warehousing, catalogues, shipping, depreciation, office supplies, postage, etc.

2. General expenses—are related to the overall operation of a business, for example, wages for officers, office staff, accounting personnel, and legal workers. Also includes fringe benefits, supplies, rent, utilities, telephone, non-sale-related travel, depreciation, postage, entertainment, and professional fees.

3. Administrative expenses—is also related to the overall operation of the business.

Chapter 14 – Statement of Cash Flows

We just went over the net income statements which represents the amount of revenue minus the cost of goods or expenses and taxes. However, the flow of cash is recorded on the statement of cash flows. This statement is the actual amount of cash the business receives and pays out. Usually with the accrual method it may cause a big difference between the income statement and the statement of cash flows.

The revenue and expense may be recognized even though the statement of cash flows does not change. The statement of cash flows will focus on three different types of activities for your business.

1. Operating activities—will relate to day-to-day operations.
2. Investing activities—will relate to long-term and some short-term assets.
3. Financing activities—will relate to shareholders, banks, investors, and liabilities.

Even though the statement of cash flows focuses on these three types it also includes two directions of cash flows.

1. Inflows—which is the cash received.
2. Outflows—which is the cash spent.

Both the inflows and outflows will change with the company's holdings in assets, liabilities, equity, and noncash assets. The statement of cash flows is a valuable tool for stakeholders. It will show the cash flow of the company and help investors make decisions for the corporation and how to use the cash that is brought in for the company.

With a statement of cash flows it also includes an investing section. This will allow investors to see how their investments are being used to grow the company. For example, if the statement of cash flows shows purchases of land or equipment it may say to the investor that the company is growing or expanding.

Another part of the statement of cash flows is the financing section. This shows how the company is borrowing money and paying off any debts.

With the statement of cash flows it can be compared from year to year. This can give you a good outlook at how the business is doing each year in comparison to the previous years.

How is the Statement of Cash Flows Used?

Now that we have some background of what a statement of cash flows is, we need to ask ourselves how it is used. When you think about it this statement has many uses, for example:

- Predicting a business or company's future cash flow
- Ability to pay dividends
- Evaluating its management decisions

Knowing that it has so many uses makes it such a vital statement to have to show the growth of the company and help make good business decisions. It is important that it is accurate and appropriate with information. A good general rule to remember is that whenever there is an inflow or outflow of cash in assets, liabilities, or equity then it should be reported on the statement of cash flows under operating activities, investing activities, or financing activities.

BALANCE SHEET CATEGORY	STATEMENT OF CASH FLOWS
Current assets (other than cash)	Operating activities
Current liabilities	Operating activities
Long-term assets	Investing activities
Long-term liabilities	Financing activities

The above chart shows how each category in the balance sheet will transfer to the statement of cash flows.

One way the statement of cash flows is used is by helping managers and investors effectively predict future cash flows. This statement will provide accurate information that is both historical and current economic. This information will show cash related to financing, investing, and operating activities. When you use this information in conjunction with budget expectations and expected income and expense information then it will help managers and investors make good and effective predictions when making decisions for the company.

Another effective use of this statement is that it helps management and outside individuals analyze the company's operating, financing, and investing activities.

If you are a public traded firm, then the statement can also help managers determine when to declare and pay dividends.

Methods of Cash Flows Reporting

There are two ways to prepare a statement of cash flows. We will first look at the direct method for reporting cash flow. It is also known as the income statement method. This method is also approved by the GAAP. This is because it converts the income statement items into cash items. It will also include receipts and cash payments in the operating activities section of the cash flows. Let's take a look at Tony's Tots comparative balance sheet for 2014 and 2015.

Comparative Balance Sheet
Tony's Tots
December 31, 2014 and 2015

	2014 amount	2015 amount	Increase (Decrease) 2014 amount-2015 amount
Assets			
Cash	$42,000	$25,000	$17,000
Accounts receivable	$26,000	$34,000	($8,000)
Inventory	$22,000	$15,000	$7,000
Property, plant, and equipment	$50,000	$78,000	($28,000)
Accumulated depreciation	($20,000)	($24,000)	$4,000
Total assets	$120,000	$128,000	($8,000)
Liabilities and equity			
Accounts payable	$12,000	$23,000	($11,000)
Income taxes payable	$13,000	$10,000	$3,000
Notes payable (long term)	$10,000	$33,000	($23,000)
Common stock	$41,000	$24,000	$17,000
Retained earnings	$44,000	$38,000	$6,000
Total liabilities and equity	$120,000	$128,000	($8,000)

Operating Activities

For us to determine the cash flows from operating activities it is necessary to calculate the cash receipts from sales, cash payments for inventory purchases, and cash payments for operating expenses.

The following formulas can be used to calculate the cash receipts.

- Cash receipts = Net sales + Decrease in accounts receivable

- Cash receipts = Net sales – Increase in accounts receivable

Next you will need to also determine the cash payments for inventory purchases. You should start with calculating the amount of purchases for the year using one of these formulas.

- Purchases = Cost of goods sold + Increase in inventory

- Purchases = Cost of goods sold – Decrease in inventory

After determining the cash payment for inventory, you will now need to determine how many of these purchases were actually paid in cash with one of the following formulas.

- Cash payments for inventory purchases = Purchases − Increase in accounts payable
- Cash payments for inventory purchases = Purchases + Decrease in accounts payable

Finally, we need to determine how much of the operating expenses are cash related. We need to deduct any noncash outflow from the amount of the operating expenses. On the income statement you will see a tax expense. This extra step will be included in the last step. Use one of the following formulas to determine this amount.

- Cash payment for income taxes = Income tax expense + Decrease in income tax payable
- Cash payment for income taxes = Income tax expense − Increase in income tax payable

Investing Activities

The primary activities in this section include cash inflows and outflows for the major fixed assets, for example, land and equipment. This will also include other types such as bonds or stock investments.

Financing Activities

This is the final section and includes all cash flows that involve borrowing money. This also includes dividend payments and selling stock for cash.

Let's take a look at a sample of the Statement of Cash Flows (direct method)

Statement of Cash Flows
Tony's Tots
2014-2015

Operating Activities
    Cash receipts from sales $358,000
    Cash payments

Inventory purchases	$298,000	
Operating expenses	$24,000	
Interest expense	$4,000	
Income taxes expense	$5,000	
Total cash outflows		$331,000
Net cash flows from operating Activities		$27,000

Investing Activities
    Sale of equipment $12,000
Net cash flows from investing
Activities $12,000

Financing Activities
    Decrease in note payable   ($23,000)
    Issuing common stock $17,000
    Dividends paid   ($16,000)
Net cash flows from financing
Activities   ($22,000)

Net cash flows for the year $17,000
Beginning cash balance $25,000
Ending cash balance $42,000

The other method for reporting is the indirect method. The only difference between the direct and the indirect methods is the operating activities. The basic rules for reconciling the accrued income to cash income for the indirect method are as follows:

- ADD depreciation expense

- ADD amortization expense

- ADD loss on sale of equipment or other investments

- SUBTRACT gain on sale of equipment or other investments

- ADD decrease in current assets

- SUBTRACT increase in current assets

- ADD increase in current liabilities

- SUBTRACT decrease in current liabilities

It does not matter which method you use. The direct and indirect methods will show the same general information.

Chapter 15 – Financial Ratios

We have covered a lot about the basics of accounting. As a bonus I wanted to add this section as a guide and a resource to you. As you progress with accounting you will soon learn that you need to analyze what is in those financial statements that we have covered and I am including statements that may be introduced to you at a later time. These ratio analyses provide another way for you to learn about the health of a company financially. Even if you do not want to work as an accountant or a bookkeeper, but yet you would like to invest your money, it is useful to know this chapter.

Even though there are many ratios that you could learn and cover I am going to focus on the five primary groups. They are:

1. Profit Ratios
2. Debt Ratios
3. Efficiency Ratios
4. Equity Ratios
5. Liquidity Ratios

Profit Ratios

A profit ratio will show how profitable a company is. This will give managers, investors, and creditors a clear picture of how well a business is doing. This is also the most frequently used group of ratios.

The operating margin ratio is the most frequently used profit ratio. It will compare the income from operations to revenue.

The operating margin is equal to a company's income from operations divided by its net sales.

- Operating margin = Income from operations / Net sale

Another type of profit ratio is the return on assets ratio. This will analyze the relationship between net income and assets used to generate the income.

- Return on assets = Net sales / {(Assets at end of year + Assets at beginning of year) / 2}

Debt Ratios

The debt ratios give valuable information about the money a company owes. They will help creditors understand what portion of the debt is current and what portion is long term. It also determines the business's level of debt compared to its equity and the relationship between the debt and revenue of the business.

The debt-to-equity ratio is a common debt ratio. This ratio is usually presented as a percentage.

- Debt-to-equity ratio = Total liabilities / Equity

Another ratio that helps banks decide if they will lend your business money is the long-term liabilities to capital ratio.

- Long-term capital structure = Long-term debt / (Long-term debt + Equity)

Efficiency Ratios

The efficiency ratios are sometimes referred to as turnover ratios. These measure how efficiently the business is using various types of assets. One of the most critical is the cash asset.

An efficiency ratio that measures the length of time to convert a sale to cash is the Days Sales Outstanding (DSO) ratio.

- DSO = (Receivables / Total credit sales) * Days in the accounting period

Keep in mind that the lower the result, the faster the company is collecting the cash it needs to sustain operations or its investments.

Equity Ratios

Equity ratios are very important for investors as they are the ones that supply equity to the corporation by purchasing stock in that company. These types of ratios will help investors decide whether they should or should not buy stock in the company.

A good ratio for this is the return on equity ratio. This will measure the relationship between net income and sales to equity.

- Return on equity = Net income / {(Equity at beginning of the year + Equity at the end of the year) / 2}

The higher the return on the equity means a better performance.

Liquidity Ratios

Businesses and companies maintain balances of liquid and long-term assets. These are to ensure their current operations and long-term financial health. Therefore, it is important that managers have a good understanding of this through liquidity ratios.

One example of these will be the current ratio. This ratio will determine if current assets cover the current liabilities. This should be greater than 1.

- Current ratio = Total current assets / Total current liabilities

Another important ratio to remember is the working capital. This ratio will show how the current assets compare to its current liabilities. This number should always be positive. However, it could also vary greatly.

- Working capital = Current assets – Current liabilities

Even though the formulas for these ratios are provided and straightforward it could be interpreted differently. Sometimes you will need to use a few different ratios to figure out how the company is doing and even more research into that company.

Conclusion

As we took this adventure into the accounting world I hope that you were able to learn some of the basics of accounting. Accounting is all around us. We use it in our everyday lives.

This has only been a brief outlook into accounting as there is so much more that can be covered. The following will give you an idea of some of the other areas you may want to venture out into:

- Tax preparation
- Computerized accounting
- Financial statement analysis
- Auditing
- Government and not-for-profit

As you can see there are so many aspects to accounting and bookkeeping. If you want to start your own business, be a bookkeeper, get a loan, or even have a bank account you should learn about this great art of numbers.